NOT SO NEW LABOUR

A sociological critique of
New Labour's policy and practice

Simon Prideaux

First published in Great Britain in March 2005 by

The Policy Press
University of Bristol
Fourth Floor
Beacon House
Queen's Road
Bristol BS8 1QU
UK

Tel +44 (0)117 331 4054
Fax +44 (0)117 331 4093
e-mail tpp-info@bristol.ac.uk
www.policypress.org.uk

British Library Cataloguing in Publication Data
A catalogue record for this book is available from the British Library.

Library of Congress Cataloging-in-Publication Data
A catalog record for this book has been requested.

ISBN 1 86134 459 7 paperback

A hardcover version of this book is also available.

Simon Prideaux is a Researcher in the Sociology and Social Policy
Department, University of Leeds.

Cover design by Qube Design Associates, Bristol.
Printed and bound in Great Britain by Hobbs the Printers, Southampton.

Contents

Acknowledgements

First of all, I would like to thank Alan Deacon, Kirk Mann and Peter Dwyer for their critical comments, encouragement and friendship during the time it has taken to produce this work. Their robust and informative opinions have been invaluable to say the least. My gratitude also extends to all those in the Sociology and Social Policy department at Leeds who have had to endure my brooding presence during the time taken to complete the necessary research and documentation. In particular, I am greatly appreciative of Moira Doolan and her constructive observations about the initial manuscript. Likewise, a special thanks goes to Jodie, Liz, Marie, Sarah and last, but by no means the least, 'Debs' in the Sociology and Social Policy office.

On the domestic front, my family have been extremely supportive through the emotional highs and lows I have experienced during the writing of this book. Specific appreciation and gratitude goes to my wife and partner, Sammy Prideaux, and to Doreen Prideaux, my mother. Credit is also due to Nicôle and Elyse-Marie Prideaux for being the children that they are.

In loving memory of Gabrielle Louise Prideaux
(1986–1987)

ONE

Introduction

This book is written from a vantage point that tends to come from below. It looks up from personal experiences, setbacks and temporary successes in the industrial world to utilise a later, more appreciative (in terms of understanding) education. As a consequence, the book questions why benign interpretations of society – and, in particular, benevolent explanations of capitalism – can be held to be true. Overall, it is believed that the experience of how social policies actually impact upon oneself and, naturally, upon others, helps to inform the stance taken throughout. Unemployment, debt, concerns over healthcare and the future education of offspring have all played their part. And it is from the basis of this platform that the book has constructed many of its arguments.

In its most rudimentary form, the central premise of this work is the conviction that New Labour, when dealing with welfare, utilise the age-old sociological diagnoses and remedies of structural-functionalism to help counter and rectify the perceived ills of contemporary British society. However, this is not to suggest that New Labour are either aware of, openly display or even acknowledge their allegiance to such trains of thought. Nor is it to suggest that functionalism is the only influence behind Labour's policies. More, it is an attempt to describe the way in which North American sociological thinking has directly or indirectly made an impact on the interpretations to which Tony Blair and his party attach to past, present and future social relations. Arguably, it is these interpretations that have led New Labour to adopt similar welfare-to-work policies as those already implemented and operational in the US; hence, the intention of this book to explore any shared theoretical foundations in an all-embracing attempt to reveal and explain the origins of the relatively pubescent 'workfare' schemes in Britain today.

Of course, the American connection with New Labour is not a particularly original theme. Only one year after Blair's election victory, Stephen Driver and Luke Martell (1998) made it quite clear that they thought New Labour were heavily influenced by events on the other side of the Atlantic. Besides comparing Labour's latest definition of social justice with the writings of Robert Reich (former Secretary of

State for Labor under former US president Bill Clinton), Driver and Martell (1998, p 57) also point out that welfare-to-work envisaged in the UK "echoes US workfare policies and has even been proposed in an Americanised 'New Deal' rhetoric by [Gordon] Brown [whereas] proposed changes to Britain's tax and benefits system is firmly based on North American experience".

Ruth Levitas (1996) also makes a connection between the two. She, like this book, acknowledges the influence of the overwhelmingly American-oriented new communitarian thinking on Labour's 'modernisers'. Likewise, she alludes to functionalism when she talks of social exclusion and 'The new Durkheimian hegemony' (Levitas, 1998). This book differs from Levitas and Driver and Martell in that the American connections will be firmly brought out in more depth. On the one hand, the functionalist focus of this book will be upon the type of sociological thinking so dominant in America during the 1950s, 1960s and early 1970s. It will not specifically relate to Durkheim, whose work was significantly altered by this American paradigm. On the other, the detected new communitarian influence will also be traced back to its North American sociological roots. Moreover, the arguments of the New Right will be brought into the debate since they can be seen either as derivatives of functionalism and communitarianism, or, at the very least, as complementary attachments to functionalist thinking and policy. Only in this way can the stage be set for the aforementioned elucidation of the theoretical roots that lay behind British welfare-to-work schemes.

Initially, Chapter Two explains what is meant by 'functionalism'. In particular, the chapter focuses upon the American based structural-functionalists and their successive constructions of society. In particular, the chapter emphasises the most prominent factors to which eminent sociologists such as Talcott Parsons (1949, 1952, 1966, 1967), Robert K. Merton (1968) and Kingsley Davis and Wilbert E. Moore (1967) attributed social cohesion and the achievement of what Émile Durkheim, as early as 1893, once described as 'organic solidarity' (Durkheim, 1933). Parsons, of course, takes centre stage. After all, it is he who is generally recognised to be the founding father of this structural form of functionalism. And, in relation to Parsons, the chapter outlines his now famous Adaptation, Goal attainment, Integration and Latency (AGIL) model and explains his meticulous interpretation of social development.

With references to the emphasis Parsons places upon how society has a natural propensity towards 'equilibrium' (Parsons et al, 1953; Parsons and Smelser, 1957) and 'evolutionary' (Parsons, 1971) transition, the chapter proceeds to examine the designated supporting roles that Parsons envisaged the family, education and work would play in the promotion and maintenance of harmonious social relations. In so doing, the chapter attempts to reveal many of the benign assumptions that Parsons and his devotees have appeared to make about society in general and the way in which the socioeconomic system of capitalism tends to work. Consequently, the final aspect of the chapter involves itself in the difficulties that such interpretations have in accounting for conflict, change and individual difference.

Moving on from this, Chapter Three shows how the functionalist leanings of Amitai Etzioni's early sociological days have influenced his present thoughts on the future development of society as a whole. Specifically, this chapter concentrates upon how organisational studies throughout the 1960s and 1970s have fundamentally restricted themselves within the confines of North American relations of capital (see Allen, 1975) and subsequently provided a myopic basis (Bauer, 1997) for the new communitarian bible, *The new golden rule* (Etzioni, 1997). It is not, however, a journey that remains confined to the work of Amitai Etzioni. As the depth of the contributions to *The essential communitarian reader* (Etzioni, 1998) illustrates, the full scope and influence of these trains of thought cannot be attributed to one individual alone.

In this respect, then, Chapter Four places Etzioni's ideas in the context of other important contributions, such as those from Philip Selznick (1953, 1994, 1998, 1999) who also happened to come from a similar sociological background. This chapter examines the work of John Macmurray (1932, 1933, 1935a, 1935b, 1961). Significantly, Tony Blair has made no secret of his admiration for the philosophical works of Macmurray. Blair openly recognises Macmurray's contribution to the understanding of the individual in society, and readily acknowledges Macmurray's overriding desire for philosophy to place individuals in their rightful social setting. Yet, Blair also views this philosophical shift as a reinforcement of modern notions of community that emphasise an obligation to others as well as to oneself (Blair in Conford, 1996). Given this, the chapter serves a broader purpose. In essence, Chapter Five provides the basis upon which the rest of the book can reveal the possibility that Blair may have misread – and therefore wrongly applied – the specific nuances that lay behind the works of Macmurray. By implication, this error in understanding could have contributed to New Labour's pursuit of a social policy direction that contradicts Macmurray's visions of capitalism and its effects upon human agency, behaviour, rationality and morality.

In order to do this, the works of Macmurray are compared with the previously cited works of Parsons and Etzioni. After careful consideration, it will become clear that Macmurray's interpretation of capitalism and that of community – especially how such a community is seen by Macmurray to operate and benefit all within – flies in the face of the constructions already put forward by Parsons and Etzioni. To fully appreciate the importance of these disparities, the rest of the chapter provides a more detailed exploration of the minutiae behind these differing explanations. As a consequence, the chapter provides a workable platform from which an informed comparison with New Labour's actual policy details (set out in Chapter Six) can be made. In short, this comparative exercise allows Chapter Seven to make a critical and informed judgement about the origins of New Labour's interpretation of capitalism, the community and the family.

In the meantime, Chapter Five introduces the notion of ideas having to appeal to different constituencies by bringing the beliefs of the New Right into the debate. To be more accurate, this chapter reverses the focus of appeal. In actual fact it is about the attraction of specific ideas to those individuals and parties in the position to adopt and implement them within the policy arena. The chapter thus introduces the pragmatic compatibility of specifically 'right-wing' ideas to the fundamental standpoint of New Labour. Consequently, arguments presented by Charles Murray (1984, 1996a, 1996b) and Lawrence Mead (1986, 1987, 1991) become central to the overall thrust of this book. On one level, their inclusion helps to further demonstrate the importation of American ideas into the British political arena. On another level, the adoption of their ideas helps to strengthen the functionality hypothesis itself. It is true that Murray, for instance, is not and does not view himself as a functionalist. Nevertheless, such a declaration fails to see how such ideas neatly fit into the functionalist interpretation of society.

Murray is a libertarian at heart yet he describes the underclass as "idle thieving bastards" (Bagguley and Mann, 1992, p 118), deliberately unwilling to work, purposely living a life of crime and intentionally having illegitimate children in order to secure social security benefits (Murray, 1984, 1986a, 1986b, 1988, 1993). It is a lifestyle that is viewed in complete contradistinction to the accepted norms of society. Therefore, Murray's recommended solution – to curtail welfare payments to these individuals – represents a move to force these people back into the sphere of social acceptability. Murray does not have to declare his allegiance to functionalist theory; his very description of the underclass itself does that for him. By implication, his description sees the good 'citizens' of this world as having to work hard, be honest and having come from a 'stable' family background. Put simply, they have to follow the functionally prescribed moral norms of society: good individuals have to be functional not dysfunctional. This, of course, neatly takes the chapter on to the work of Mead. It is he who expounds upon the work of Murray, and it is he who directly relates to the functionality/dysfunctionality hypothesis when talking of the underclass. Consequently, it is through this channel that the chapter can accommodate the works of Charles Murray and the New Right into the functionalist leanings of New Labour and its attempt to change the culture perceived to exist among benefit claimants (Government Green Paper, 1998b).

With Chapter Six, the book begins to demonstrate, on the one hand, how all these strands have begun to reinforce and promote functionalist trains of thought and, on the other, how they have become manifest in the social policies of New Labour. Initially, the chapter approaches this synthesis through a discussion of the ideas of Tony Blair's acknowledged guru, Anthony Giddens, and his now famous conception of the 'third way' (1998a, 2000) that goes 'beyond left and right' (1994, 1998b). On closer inspection, the chapter manages to reveal that, by giving primacy to the provision of 'opportunity', Giddens opens up an initial connection with the structural-functionalism of Parsons, Merton and Davis and Moore which was discussed in Chapter Three. Moving on, the chapter notes that the similarities in language and policy proposals of the 'third way' also tends to have an affinity with Chapter Four's discussion of the organisational and communitarian deliberations of Amitai Etzioni.

From the platform of this form of logic, the chapter essentially argues that Gordon Brown and others were able to postulate that the welfare state could and should be reorganised to provide 'pathways' out of unemployment, poverty and, ultimately, crime (Brown, 1994, pp 4-5). Undeniably, it was believed that with this reorganisation the disadvantaged, the single parent and the long-term unemployed would be able to meet both society's and their own personal 'motivational needs' as they pass through avenues of opportunity and so lighten a perceived burden on the welfare state. In this respect, the chapter gives pride of place to the part the multifarious New Deal schemes have to play in this reorganisation of welfare in Britain today. Indeed, the ensuing discussion of the actual details of these schemes serves to cement further the connection between New Labour and functionalist interpretations of society.

Yet, as the remarks of Chapter Seven postulate, perhaps this embodiment of the benign functionalist ideal of capitalism and the elusive 'American dream' gives too much faith to those having to strive for success within the highly competitive free market that New Labour aspires to stimulate (Labour Party, 2003). Prominently, the chapter demonstrates that New Labour, like the early functionalists before it, has neglected to heed any of the forebodings Macmurray (1935a, 1935b, 1950, 1961), to name but one, had about the destructive machinations of capitalism. In relation to this neglect, the book comes to a close with the tentative suggestion that it may well be possible for the same Achilles heel of benign interpretation (which eventually proved to be the demise of the sociological discipline of structural-functionalism) could re-emerge to bedevil the welfare policies now put in place by New Labour. Certainly, the emergent tensions and contradictions described in this final chapter could suggest that these misgivings are beginning to come to fruition.

TWO

Functionalism and society: Talcott Parsons and the American hegemony in sociology

An introduction to structural-functionalism

The purpose and relevance of this chapter is twofold. First, it is a chapter that helps to make a clear distinction between 'functionality' and the form of 'functionalism' underpinning the policies of New Labour. Second, the chapter also aims to provide a focus that will enable the book to portray a working and detailed definition of the 'functionalism' utilised by New Labour. Through this definition, it will then be possible for the book to make a clear separation of policies that are functional (that is, those that are practical) from those that draw from functionalist trains of thought (in other words, policies premised upon a benign, teleological view of society and capitalism in particular). Both aspects are integral parts of the policy-making process employed by New Labour. Certainly it is true that all governments intend to introduce policies that are 'designed' to serve a function. It would be illogical and politically damning to do otherwise. Nonetheless, the benevolent impression of capitalism – so reminiscent of the functionalism popularised in the US from the 1930s on – can still be seen in much of New Labour's policy direction.

To begin with, the main concentration of this chapter is upon what Richard Kilminster (1998) once described as a monopoly phase in British and American sociology. During the period 1945-65, he identified a "domination of the paradigm of structural functionalism deriving from Talcott Parsons and Robert K. Merton" (1998, p 154). It was the work of these two eminent sociologists that helped to establish a supposed synthesis of the works of Durkheim, Weber, Pareto and Freud that, despite its demise and apparent dismissal in the 1970s, still exerts an influence upon contemporary sociology and social policy. Most notably, it was the continuing work of Parsons that provided the initial platform for Kingsley Davis and Wilbert E. Moore (1967) to complete a short, highly influential sociological study of stratification upon which Merton (1968) was able to elaborate and expand. As we shall see in due course, the resultant social model produced has a particular relevance to this book in that it provides a framework of reference that easily relates to the theoretical underpinnings used to substantiate and justify the British welfare reforms of today.

In its most sophisticated Parsonian form, this structural-functionalism:

> stressed that society as a social system of interrelated parts, survived because it evolved institutional structures to fulfil the basic needs of the system, its 'functional prerequisites'. In focusing on social order, integration and the stability of the system achieved via people internalising commonly held values, functionalism had a reputation ... for providing an essentially harmonious, stabilising model of the whole society. (Kilminster, 1998, p 154)

In a way, one could argue that these considerations of the structural-functionalists in the 'Pareto Circle', as they have become known, were an expression of what they saw as the realities of the great 'American dream', a dream in which the 'rags to riches' scenario was made possible and accessible.

After all, capitalism was a system that had survived longer than any other and the US version had been relatively successful for the likes of Parsons and his former student, Merton. Undoubtedly, they had reached positions of responsibility and esteem within America's academic community. Possibly, some of the consequences of this were that notions of conflict, struggle and the often insurmountable obstacles to social progression had very little relevance in their sociological examination of the world they lived in. In contrast, social equilibrium (which to these successful functionalists was a significant feature of their society) provided the key to cohesion and happiness. Effectively, American structural-functionalists saw the US version of capitalism as the ideal form of social relations. However, it was not the capitalism that others saw. Rather, it was a benign social pyramid of opportunity which, through motivational competition and the free-market economy, satiated aspiration and duly rewarded the individual for their endeavour.

With this in mind, it comes of little surprise that the emergence and dominance of this sociological paradigm in the US and Britain actually coincided with a global period "of American economic, military and cultural domination of Europe, as well as of the confrontation between West and East – the cold war" (Kilminster, 1998, p 154). The inference from this, of course, being that many of these social commentators had a vested reason to depict Western, and in particular US, society as superior to the equivalent Eastern, Warsaw-Pact versions. In actual fact, it is an inference that has led William Buxton (1985, p 4) to assert that:

> Parsonian theory was not so much an attempt to describe an externalised reality, as it was an effort ... directed towards elaborating how a more integrated social order – one preserving capitalist social relations, yet providing them with stability – could be constituted.

Indeed, Parsons' residual commitment to socialism during his stay at the London School of Economics (LSE) (1924-25) had, by the 1930s if not earlier, become subsumed by an appointment to Harvard (1927) and a greater appreciation of market forces. Socialist planning, in the eyes of Parsons, could not substitute for markets without involving considerable losses in efficiency and a loss of both an individual and national capacity to create wealth. To this end, during the Great Depression, Parsons gave avid support for Roosevelt's New Deal as he looked towards a better regulation of capitalism and a concomitant "expansion of a prosperous middle class as the most effective way to pursue values of social equality" (Lidz, 2003, p 380). In essence, a concern grew over how the American nation-state could be consolidated and subsequently promoted "as a prototype for global social reform" (Buxton, 1985, p 4).

Nevertheless, this is not to suggest that all functionalists can be tarred with the same brush. In this respect, it is important to distinguish the radical socio-functionalists of the Chicago School (see Park, 1950), for instance, from the 'Pareto Circle' in order to provide clarity of focus upon the brand of structural-functionalism this book is concerned with. Thus, the Chicago School have to be acknowledged in (yet excluded from) a more detailed discussion, for it was they who attempted to diagnose the problems of squalor, poverty and deviant behaviour within American society. They, at least, recognised the problems that exist within, and arguably arise out of, contemporary societal structures premised upon relations of capital. Similarly, Emile Durkheim, the supposed founding father of this structural-functionalism, should also be excluded from these ranks. Apart from the obvious generational difference, he too recognised the fact that modern society is problematic. Why else would he concentrate on the causes of suicide? Why else would Durkheim (2002, p 350) investigate the anomic condition that "springs from the lack of collective forces at certain points in society"? Despite this, it is still safe to conclude that the sociological considerations of Talcott Parsons managed to meet with an unprecedented amount of acclaim for a social commentator of our more contemporary times. On this basis alone, the considerable work of Parsons is deserving of a more detailed examination.

Who killed Herbert Spencer?

In his most famous introductory work, *The structure of social action* (first published in 1937), Talcott Parsons (1902-1979) asked, "Who now reads Spencer?" (Parsons, 1949, p 3). When asking this, Parsons was conveying his admiration for Herbert Spencer (1820-1903) who was one of the few sociologists that could rival Marx "in intellectual influence in the nineteenth century" (Turner, 2003, p 69). In particular, Parsons was expressing a fascination for Spencer's ability to replicate economic theory and the "neat and abstract way in which economists explain human behaviour" (Hamilton, 1983, p 66). For Parsons, the elegance of economic theory was its ability to strip away any non-rational aspect of human action in its portrayal of economic activity (Parsons, 1934b). Likewise, Spencer's sociology attempted to provide a grand abstract system derived from a notion of 'social evolution' that stretched in an unbroken chain of development from primitive man to contemporary industrialised society. In short, Spencer believed that his concept of 'social evolution' provided the means to progressively uncover "human rationality from its shroud of ignorance, superstition and fear" (Hamilton, 1983, p 66).

Yet strangely, in the light of a number of accusations of positivism and behaviourism levelled at his later works (Hamilton, 1985), Parsons went on to ask "who killed him [Spencer] and how?" (Parsons, 1949, p 3). In asking this question, Parsons was reflecting an initial uncertainty over the positivistic assumptions that Spencer had made about human behaviour within his 'evolutionary' theory. Effectively, Spencer's deliberations had subsumed the feelings, values, beliefs and knowledge of an individual into an overly simplistic model of rule-following activities (Hamilton, 1983). In contrast, during this stage of his sociological career, Parsons saw that the rational means–ends schema of economic theory could not always provide a complete and incontrovertible theory of societal development and human action. Rather, sociological variables had to be invoked. Sociology had to move away from Spencer's utilitarian attempts to answer questions over the origins and future of human society. Instead, sociology, in

Parsons' mind (1949, p 768), should turn its attention towards developing "an analytic theory of social action systems in so far as these systems can be understood in terms of the property of common value integration". In other words, the aim of sociology in Parsons' eyes was to produce an overarching demonstration of social action that demonstrates its structure and meaning through theories that order the chaos of individual experience (Hamilton, 1983).

Without doubt, Parsons, even in these formative years, was primarily concerned with the problems of social order. At first, he was preoccupied with the means to explain how social order came about. Later, in texts such as *The social system* (1952), Parsons was obsessed with the conundrum of how individuals, defined as separate entities pursuing their self-interest, avoid a life of chaos and disorder. How are human groups or societies able "to achieve as much stability as they do, how [are] their component parts … integrated in such a way as to minimise disruptive conflict?" (Johnson, 1975, pp 10-11). In reality, of course, disorder is not the case. People do cooperate and people do integrate with each other, hence the conundrum.

In an attempt to resolve this dilemma, Parsons initially believed that the basis of social integration must arise out of the values of society and its 'social actors'. Social action, as a form of 'voluntarism' where people act on the basis of their own values and the values and norms of people around them, represents the key to the puzzle. Actions do not occur "singly and discretely, they are organised in systems" (Parsons, 1952, p 7) that constrict an actor as he, or she, utilises both the 'ends' and the 'means' of acts which are themselves socially derived from daily routines. 'Ends', he noted, are based upon shared values and norms that are "internalised in the motivational systems of individuals" (Johnson, 1993, quoted in Gingrich,1999a, p 5) whereas the 'means' "that people use are socially and morally regulated, with views of right and wrong, proper and improper, and appropriate and not" (Gingrich, 1999b, p 5).

However, this was only a small part of a much larger picture. Integral to Parsons' overarching theory was the notion that social action occurs within a social system of mutually dependent parts that contribute to the functioning of the system in a moving equilibrium where disturbance induces a counter-reaction to maintain social balance and order (Cuneo, 2000). In the language of Parsons (1952, pp 5-6), a social system thus:

> consists in a plurality of individual actors interacting with each other in a situation which has at least a physical or

environmental aspect, actors who are motivated in terms of a tendency to the 'optimisation of gratification' and whose relation to their situations, including each other, is defined and mediated in terms of a system of culturally structured and shared symbols.

Quite clearly, Parsons was relating, on the one hand, to an individual tendency to seek personal satisfaction and, on the other, to a mutually supportive process of socialisation arising out of life in the family, school, work and the community at large. Yet these two aspects become one and the same since it is through this process that the individual learns the values and norms of a society, and it is through this learning that an individual becomes bound to the social system by seeking a revised personal gratification based upon internalised social expectations and customs. In his own inimitable way, Parsons (1952, p 37) expressed this internalisation of motives and goals by insisting that it is important to:

> distinguish between the attitude of 'expediency' at one pole, where conformity or non-conformity is a function of the instrumental interests of the actor, and at the other pole the 'introjection' ... of the standard so that to act in conformity with it becomes a need-disposition in the actor's own personality structure, relatively independently of any instrumentally significant consequences of that conformity.

From this vantage point, it is still apparent that Parsons was holding on to elements of action theory even if it purported only a limited scope for individual agency outside of the socialisation process.

AGIL, pattern maintenance and institutionalisation

With his later theoretical deliberations, however, Parsons began to undermine the importance of individual action altogether. A more familiar version of structural-functionalism began to arise. Later, in the *Working papers in the theory of action* (Parsons et al, 1953) individuals, and subsequently the various social processes and social institutions in which individuals participate, became integrated components in the successful operation of society as a system. In other words, an individual's ability to act independently became subsumed by a perceived function to contribute to "a complex set of activities directed towards meeting a need or needs of the system" (Rocher, 1975, in

Ritzer, 2000, p 441). As a consequence, patterns of association and action merely reflected an accepted, working consensus of activity that significantly reinforced and added to what Parsons identified as the structurally 'functional imperatives' of adaptation (A), goal attainment (G), integration (I) and latency or pattern maintenance (L) – hence, AGIL (Parsons et al, 1953).

Crucially, it was through this AGIL model of social structures that Parsons began to build an organic vision of a successful social structure and its workings. Like the organs within a living creature, each sphere and the activities within it were deemed to be essential for the maintenance and well-being of the whole. So, in the Parsonian scheme of things, a social system or subsystem could only flourish if the four prerequisites of the AGIL acronym were met. The first two of which, were necessary for the survival and continued operation of the system as a whole (Gingrich, 1999b). Explicitly, they referred to instrumental activity whereby adaptive "behaviour on the part of the actor is carried on in conjunction with goal-attainment by the collectivity" (Bourricaud, 1981, p 88). By contrast, the last two were concerned with establishing group solidarity (Bourricaud, 1981) and were also seen to effectively act as a means to regulate the social system (Gingrich, 1999b).

From this general perspective, *adaptation*, for instance, related to economic facilities and, as such, "is a dimension that represents the forces in the social system closest to the material world, i.e., the coercive, 'conditional' forces which must be faced and adapted to whether people like it or not" (Alexander, 1987, p 92). With the *goal attainment element*, however, the main focus was upon the political functions of society (Parsons, 1985a). Politics and government were most clearly associated with this subsystem yet they were not coterminous. In a sense, this part of the model was also influenced by adaptive, material concerns. Consequently, 'organisation' – with its attempt "to control the impact of external forces in order to achieve carefully delimited goals" (Alexander, 1987, p 92) – represented the key to survival and success. In short, Parsons saw that the aim of this sphere was to utilise 'power' (as distinct from wealth) in order to maximise the capacity of a society to attain its systemic or collective goals (Parsons, 1985a).

At the other end of the scale, *integration* took the model into the realms of the church, courts, police and the law. This was the sphere of Parsons' model that concerned itself with the establishment of norms and the regulation of social relationships and interrelationships. Put simply, these 'integrative' mechanisms were the Parsonian equivalent of what many sociologists would refer to as the instruments of social control (Parsons, 1985a). In this context, integration had two distinct forms. The first was deemed to define the limits of 'permissiveness' in relation to individuals and groups during social change. For Parsons, successful integration "involves a determinate set of relations among member units of the system such that it retains and reinforces its boundary-maintaining character as a single entity" (Parsons et al, 1953, p 184). Consequently, during social change, the integrative sphere regulates the allocation of goods, services, responsibilities and even people in order to maintain the overall integrity of the system. Concurrently, the second aspect of social control concerns the institutionalisation of what Parsons had earlier defined as the "dominant patterns of value-orientation" (Parsons, 1952, p 168). In effect, this second form of integration involves the defining of responsibility, leadership and representation on both an informal and formal level. Significantly, it was the integration element of the AGIL acronym that was seen by Parsons, on the one hand, to promote long-term attachment to the system (Lidz, 2003) and, on the other, to manage the relationship of the other three 'functional imperatives' of A, G and L (Ritzer, 2000).

Finally, *latency*, a sphere that Parsons also refers to as the cultural-motivational system (Parsons, 1967), represented the most purely subjective forces in society. Latency was "the sphere of general values that bear sufficient relation to objective concerns to be institutionalised" (Alexander, 1987, p 93). Thus, in the Parsonian scheme of things, these general values were conceived as latent functions designed to "furnish, maintain, and renew both the motivation of individuals and the cultural patterns that create and sustain ... motivation" (Ritzer, 2000, p 441) within a collectivity. Interestingly, Parsons used the term 'latency' because the function that this sphere serves is not always as apparent as the A, G or I functions. This, though, should not undermine the importance and efficacy of the sphere. For Parsons, it was crucial for social scientists to recognise that:

> cognitive meanings of particular objects must be organised in a more or less coherent system in the relations between the adaptive and latency aspects of the system. On the other hand the new cathectic meanings must be integrated into a system of possessions and assimilated to the integrative patterns of the system. Finally, both types of integration of discrete meanings meet in the latency cell to form a single ... 'value system' ... internalised or institutionalised in so far as there is 'commitment' to conformity with its norms so that performance tends to modify the situation in conformity with these norms. (Parsons et al, 1953, p 228)

Setting aside the circularity of the argument and, of course, the difficulties encountered with Parsons' language, it becomes possible to discern that the references to norms, assimilation, integration, institutionalisation and internalisation relate back to the earlier importance and relevance Parsons had given to the process of socialisation in *The social system* (1952). And in relation to the overall thrust of this book, further discussions will reveal that the Parsonian interpretation of how individuals are 'fruitfully' socialised or absorbed into a society provide a consistent frame of reference for the ensuing social commentaries provided by, first the organisational school of thought and, later, by the new communitarian movement of today.

Equilibrium, evolutionary transition and the generalised media of interchange

However, a more detailed examination of the reasoning behind the AGIL model is needed before the connections with organisational theory can be fully explored. Indeed, a closer examination of the acronym inevitably reveals some extraordinary examples of personal supposition that underpin the model's efficacy. Of prime importance was Parsons' (1991, p 41) belief that in "any given social system which is subjected to technical analysis, there is a presumption in favour of the existence and importance of a single unified value system at the requisite level of generality".

Consequently, the AGIL model was constructed to explain the "complex of normative cultural patterns which define desirable states" (Parsons, 1991, p 37) in the social system of America. In order to achieve this, the AGIL model had to be a fluid, mutually supportive framework so that it could provide a suitable basis for the classification and analysis of what Parsons believed to be the most successful, functional social structure of his day. For Parsons, a vibrant and efficient social system similar to the one in America could not remain in stasis. A successful system had to have a dynamic propensity towards equilibrium. In this respect, Parsons was obliged to recognise that transitional upheaval represented a real possibility. Without equivocation, Parsons, when collaborating with Neil Smelser (1957, p 248), declared major changes could:

> involve periods of disequilibrium and/or unstable equilibrium. The criterion of an unstable state is that even a small relevant departure from such a state leads not to tendencies to restore the original state, but to depart from

it further. Such departure continues until a different state
of relatively stable equilibrium is attained.

Yet in general, change (as experienced by a successful system) would
essentially be benign. Disruption would be minimal, and change would
follow the A to G to I to L route towards transformation (Parsons et al,
1953).

In sum, Parsons believed that transition would initially manifest itself
through a phase of orientation (*adaptation*) whereas an emphasis upon
suggestion and tension release (*goal gratification*) would soon follow.
Finally, a "last minute touch of *integration* (emphasis on solidarity)"
(1953, p 188) would enable the system to re-establish the natural state
of equilibrium reflected in "the relative 'before' and 'after' quiescence"
(p 186) of the latency dimension. Once achieved, the system would
then experience a period of 'pattern maintenance' whereby the values
transmitted in L help to support, fortify and at times regulate the
norms of I and vice versa. Similarly, L could directly limit the pursuit
of destructive goals in G or restrict any overambitious economic
pursuits encapsulated in A. Alternatively, L could fortify all of the
other three spheres at once through the promotion of a 'work ethic'
that may, ultimately, be rewarded in the economy (Alexander, 1987).

Even from this brief exposé of Parsons' thoughts on social
equilibrium, it becomes plain that this attempt to explain change within
and without social systems was premised upon an evolutionary model
of development. Nonetheless, the emphasis placed upon equilibrium
stresses (through the suggestion of graduated acquiescence) that this
evolution is not of the kind envisaged by Charles Darwin (1809-82).
As the conclusion to this chapter will reinforce, the idea of the 'survival
of the fittest' (Darwin, 1859) certainly does not spring to mind. Conflict
(in the form of revolution or at least social unrest), mutation as manifest
in the guise of unintended consequences (Willis, 1977; Elias, 1984),
or domination and submission (as in power struggles) appear to have
little if any relevance to the deliberations of Parsons. By contrast, a
model based on the musings of Jean-Baptiste Lamarck (1744-1829)
has been applied and, in this respect, development has been depicted
in an unrealistically benevolent way.

What little change that does occur tends, in the main, to have taken
a more linear trajectory in its path towards assimilation and utility.
Under these conditions, change was thus seen to be readily absorbed
into a social system with the minimum of disruption. Lamarck's (1873)
notion of an evolutionary path of adaptation appears to have dominated.
Indeed, Ritzer (2000, p 451) points out that Parsons had, by 1966,

characteristically developed his own 'paradigm of evolutionary change'. Through the passage of time, it was argued, a social structure develops and differentiates new subsystems that replace older subsystems as the new prove, in terms of both their structure and function, to have more adaptive worth to the larger society within which it operates. "If differentiation is to yield a balanced, more evolved system", argued Parsons (1966, p 22), then:

> each newly differentiated substructure ... must have increased adaptive capacity for performing its *primary* function, as compared to the performance of *that* function in the previous, more diffuse structure....We may call this process the *adaptive upgrading* aspect of the evolutionary change cycle.

Unmistakably, this is a highly positive model of social change (Ritzer, 2000). Certainly, the notion of 'adaptive upgrading', to which Parsons was to return in 1971, epitomises the benign nature of Parsons' thought process. It appears as though subsystems can be harmlessly replaced in much the same way as a car can be exchanged for a newer, faster and shinier model. To compound issues, the social system is almost rendered human when transition is depicted as deliberate and planned in a manner that suggests a social system has the ability to think and evaluate. Moreover, despite tentative acknowledgements of the less than catastrophic possibility that social structures may undergo evolutionary strain (Parsons, 1966, 1971), elements of struggle, upheaval and/or conflict are conspicuously noticeable by their absence.

Parsons continued with this rather placid theme. In a symposium convened by Peter Blau (1975), Parsons proceeded to outline what he had come to see as the functions of money, power, influence and value-commitments. For Parsons, these four 'functionaries' constituted what he coined to be the 'generalised symbolic media of interchange' where each assumes the task of mediation within multifarious social relations and interactions. Money, he argued, finds its 'home' in the economic sphere (A) of the AGIL model; power's home was designated to be in the field of polity (G), whereas influence was deemed to relate to integration (I) and, sequentially, value-commitment was integral to pattern maintenance (L) (Parsons, 1971; Lidz, 1991).

Although Parsons did not confine his discussions to money alone, he did, nonetheless, view money as the primary model to work from (Parsons, 1971, 1985b). Consequently, references to the way in which money was seen by Parsons to operate within a social structure act as a guide to how the other media symbols function. Power, for instance, "was conceived of as defining the generalised value of political resources" in much the same way as money "provides the measure of value for all economic goods that enter exchange" (Lidz, 1991, p 112). In a similar vein, influence was perceived to act as an index to integrative value. Yet for the more discerning, it is glaringly obvious that power and influence cannot be numerically quantified. Naturally, Parsons was acutely aware of this. And because of this fact, Parsons rested his argument upon the belief that members of society routinely make common-sense judgements as to who is the most powerful or influential and who is the least. Likewise, individuals make decisions as to how much power or influence they are willing to expend in given situations (Lidz, 1991).

All the same, by adopting this line of argument, Parsons was not only assuming that individuals had access to power and influence (let alone money), but was also assuming that these said individuals were freely able to dispense and acquire such resources at their beck and call. Clearly, iniquity or disparity of distribution of these 'media of interchange' did not constitute a major consideration for Parsons. Just as poignant was the use of the word 'interchange' itself. Crucially, the term explicitly relates to mutuality and, as such, generates images of alternate succession along the lines of a free-flowing traffic junction frequented by polite and considerate motorists.

Parsons was not deterred from pursuing his analysis of the symbolic character of these resources of mediation. Without going into the intricacies of the symbolic nature of money in particular, it is sufficient at this juncture to outline what Parsons saw as the four main characteristics of the symbolic media of exchange in general. That said, the constraints of time and space render a full examination impracticable. As an alternative, concentration in this book will be on money and power alone. In this respect, the first characteristic identified by Parsons was that of *institutionalisation*. With regard to money, this conceptualisation referred to the relation money tends to have with property and the fact that money receives the support of governmental authority through its status of 'legal' tender (Parsons, 1985b). Power, on the other hand, was viewed as institutionalised through its legitimisation. In terms of the political context:

> the paramount institutional complex is what we call authority. This may be defined as the legitimised capacity to make and to contribute to the implementation of decisions which are binding on a specifiable collective unit

or class of them, where the holder of authority has some
kind of right of speaking in the name of the collectivity.
(Parsons, 1985b, p 183)

Apart from being a rather vague and circular argument, Parsons is
again guilty of being a little too positive in his outlook. Corruption or
misuse of power was not a major issue for him. In actual fact, when
discussing the illegitimate use of money through the act of political
bribery, Parsons simply viewed such acts as "special cases rather than
constitutive criteria of the phenomena" (1985b, p 181). To make matters
worse, there is little understanding of what Steven Lukes (1974, p 23)
described as the "supreme exercise of power"; that is, to covertly control
and shape the thoughts of others in order to get them to do (or accept)
what you want them to. What Parsons failed to recognise was that a
position of 'authority' (as he described it) would simply make this
'supreme exercise' more possible, even tenable.

Moving on, however, the second characteristic of Parsons' account
of a media's symbolic status was that of *specificity*, by which he meant
specificity of meaning. With regard to money, Parsons argued (1985b,
p 181), money was the medium that operates in economic exchanges
yet it cannot mediate "many other interchange relations among
humans". By contrast, the arguments relating to power were twofold
and less clear. First, the concept of power, and political power in
particular, was placed by Parsons in its collective context and was used
to designate the capacity to act with authority upon the affairs
specifically relating to the collective system as a whole. Allied to this
loose attempt to contextualise power was Parsons' second ingredient,
'bindingness' (Parsons, 1967, 1985b). 'Bindingness' in the context of
power was deemed to relate to obligations and, as such, related back to
the aforementioned discussions of legitimacy and authority. In short,
Parsons decreed that the specificity of power concerns the 'collective
reference' and its concomitant justification given through a consensus
of the members of the collective. More poignantly, "authority is the
institutionalised code within which the 'language of power' is
meaningful and, therefore, ... accepted in the requisite community"
(Parsons, 1967, p 331), hence the specificity encapsulated in Parsons'
use of 'bindingness'.

In a comparatively convenient rebuff to possible accusations of
selective bias and optimism, Parsons attempted to address the problem
of the possible (but, in his opinion, the highly improbable) misuse of
power in his vision of a cohesive and efficient structure of capitalism.
If, for instance, there was the uncharacteristic event where authority

was being wielded in the form of coercion or of compulsion without justification/legitimation, then this phenomenon should not, he vehemently stipulated, be considered to be a representative example of the use of power. Rather, the loss of specificity (through the use of force and subsequently the loss of consensus) would deem an act of this kind to be an act of 'intrinsic instrumentality' designed to secure compliance rather than obligation. Consequently in Parsons' eyes, this would not be an exercise of power. Instead, it would be the political equivalent of monetary metal being used "as an instrument of barter where as a commodity it ceases to be an institutionalised medium of exchange at all" (Parsons, 1967, p 331). Thus the negative possibilities were avoided or dismissed by denial.

The third aspect of the symbolic character of these 'generalised media' was that of *circulability*. Like with commodities, observed Parsons, money changes hands (1985b, p 181). Without doubt, this tends to be the general case within Western democracies. But even then, it is noticeable that a full discussion relating to iniquities of exchange was being avoided by Parsons. Furthermore, when the discussion turned to power, the line taken was even less precise and not as apparent. Arguably, the notion of power circulating or at least being diffused *throughout* the societal collectivity seemed (and seems still) a tad too hopeful to be true. Not all members, it has to be said, can be assumed to be in a position to access and utilise power in any meaningful way. Nevertheless, Parsons attempted to counter this with reference to the existence of organisations. It was through organisations, he argued, that power was effectively operating as a circulating medium. In this sense, continued Parsons, it was the big organisations such as governments, productive enterprises and trade unions that stood out copiously. While on a smaller scale, he hastened to add (1967, p 290), "families, even friendship cliques and many other groups also have some power".

Significantly, for Parsons, it was the modern, American form of pluralism that acted as a catalyst for the circulation of power. Although the scale of organisation is large, he mused, there are many – even among large organisations – that are relatively independent of one another. However, this independence is not assumed to be absolute. Nor was it assumed by Parsons that this was a prerequisite for pluralism. Rather, Parsons (1967, p 290) believed there was "a shading from the very large through many intermediate grades to the very small". Moreover, government was deemed to be splintered (especially in the US) and definitely not monolithic. Likewise, he argued, the same held true for many large private organisations. As a consequence, the 'power structure' of these organisations (private or public) rested in a more or less stable and shifting equilibrium. And with this shifting equilibrium, circulation was seen to operate:

> through exchanges of commitments of resources and of opportunities for their utilisation, through giving and withdrawing support for various collective goals, and through the decisions that signify commitment – not only of mobile resources, but of organisations themselves. (Parsons, 1967, p 290)

Essentially, Parsons set the circulation of power in the context of amiable relations. Circulation came about through the reciprocal process of 'give and take'. It was not a question of the most powerful taking and taking alone. For Parsons, that would not represent 'circulability', and therefore was not a relevant area for discussion. Indeed, Parsons ends his discussion on the circulation of power by adding that individuals have plural memberships of organisations and collectivities, hence the circulation increases as membership spreads.

Parsons did briefly acknowledge the negative aspect of plurality being unevenly spread throughout the population of his prime example, the US. Yet, apart from alluding to the possibility that spread of membership can result in power imbalances, increased conflict within and between the various affiliations and the creation of a "delicate equilibrium among such loyalties" (1967, p 190), the acknowledgement went no further. In a similar vein, the fourth property of a 'generalised media of interchange', that a medium "could not have a zero-sum character attributed to it" (1985b, p 181), was also lacking a more comprehensive explanation.

Returning to the medium of money, Parsons pointed out that money did not have a 'zero-sum character' simply because of the economic phenomenon known as 'credit creation'. Put simply, what Parsons was refuting was the notion that, for instance, an increase in wealth on behalf of one party automatically results in a decrease of wealth on behalf of another. This, of course, is clearly not the case. The correlation is obviously not so direct. Wealth can be created and distributed. New money can be produced in the form of credit by banks and other financial institutions. Whether it is distributed fairly is another matter and, in characteristic fashion, does not enter into the debate as far as Parsons was concerned at this juncture.

In relation to power, however, Parsons began his analogy by questioning the belief that there is a fixed quantity of power within any relational system. Although Parsons admitted that there are certain circumstances where a gain of power by A, for example, could result in a corresponding diminution for the other units of B, C and D, this did not, in his opinion (1967, p 299), generally hold true for "total systems of a sufficient level of complexity". On the contrary, Parsons believed that political power in particular actually mirrors the banking parallel when power is exercised within complex societies similar to the US.

Political leaders, he pointed out, will make promises, but fulfilment of these promises remains dependent upon the implied consent of their constituencies who grant them power through election to office. Once in office, maintained Parsons, these leaders (or power holders, as he preferred to call them) may introduce more extensive plans that can only be fully implemented through the renewal and increase of political power over time. Like a bank loan, total repayment will not be immediate but will be met in the long term. Effectively, Parsons argued (1985b, p 186) that these leaders would be using their "fiduciary position" to extend their political 'credit' for politically significant enterprises that would not be politically effective in the short term.

Once again the argument is beset with the same problems. Harmonious relations of equilibrium tend to predominate the discussion. Political decisions are balanced with support from the constituencies, whereas negative factors such as political corruption, political incompetence and political deceit tend not to enter into Parsons' considerations. Instead, we get a reiteration of all the positive aspects relating to the overarching American system of capital. Almost as if Parsons were attempting to underline the point, it seems highly significant that he used money – and, indeed, credit – as the primary examples of a 'generalised medium of interchange'. In making the inextricable link between money, power and (to a lesser extent) influence, Parsons was inevitably reinforcing his undeniable admiration of the American social system and that of capitalism in general.

Institutional roles for the family, education and the workplace

In spite of the difficulties encountered with the complicated use of language, and despite the intricate application of theoretical models, it should now be evident that Parsons was charting a path of social development and social functioning that would become the platform upon which others would build. Of critical importance is the stance taken towards capitalism as a social system and the standard sociological themes that are beginning to emerge from the ensuing discussion.

The importance given to roles and functions of organisations, for instance, led to the development of organisational theory and the highly influential new communitarian movement of today (as Chapter Three of this book demonstrates). Similarly, the inference so far that the family and friendship cliques have institutionalising and socialising roles to play has to be explored in more depth in order to show how the devotees and pupils of Parsons used his deliberations to build a model of society that would, after a degree of discernment from the social commentaries of Etzioni (1995, 1997, 1998) and Giddens (1994, 1998a, 2000), provide New Labour with a theoretical basis from which it could launch many of its social policy initiatives.

In this respect, it is essential to reiterate that the sociological investigations of Parsons tended to take an optimistic stance in relation to the functions and attributes pertaining to societal structures and the subsystems, institutions and organisations contained within. The negative aspects of conflict, oppression through the misuse of power and the social iniquities in the American form of capitalism are given little attention or consideration. Although this outlook laid Parsons open to accusations of selective 'amnesia' (Mills, 1959, p 48), his persistent pursuit of the positive still remained. And this was particularly true of the way in which he envisaged the family, the educational system and the workplace acting in support of the overarching social structure of capitalism.

As mentioned earlier in this chapter, integral to Parsons' 'pattern maintenance' sphere, was the process of socialisation. Of primary importance in this respect was the institution of the family. Indeed, Parsons envisaged kinship as a major functionary in this realm (Parsons, 1952, 1967, 1971; Parsons et al, 1953). With regard to the previously discussed AGIL analogy, Parsons placed the activities of the family within the latency sphere of the social structure. In this respect, family functions were assumed to be latent because the family, as a unit, does not significantly contribute to the economic production of society. Nor was it seen to take political responsibility even though its members as individuals may do so. Instead, it was envisaged that the family only affected the other subsystems of society (such as A, G and I) indirectly. In other words, it was argued by Parsons et al (1953) that the family took responsibility for the development of the personalities of its members. In this respect, the essential focus of the family had to be that of the "ascriptive-expressive" (1953, p 267) whereby the individual is first treated in terms of their status as family members and, second, in terms of the "diffuse quality patterns of his [sic] 'social personality' of which age and sex are primary foci" (1953, p 267).

Significantly, it was in this area that Parsons' social conservatism came to the fore, particularly in relation to the family form and the role of women. In spite of a 1971 concern over the strain being placed upon the nuclear family through their growing commitments to work and school, Parsons (1971, p 101) crystallised his opinions with the statement that such "developments have placed considerable strain upon the house-wife, who must be increasingly self-reliant in fulfilling her obligations to her husband and children".

There is little doubt here that Parsons had reified the gender roles of the 1950s and, to make matters worse, had not really anticipated any changes to the contrary (Lidz, 2003).

Clearly, 'housekeeping' and child-rearing were, in the mind of Parsons, the principal roles for women to undertake. In an earlier discussion of 'parental roles', Parsons took this subjugation of women a step further with the stipulation that the adult masculine role is less "implicated with detailed child care than the feminine, and is more implicated with prestige and responsibility in the wider society and beyond the narrow kinship circle" (1952, p 222). Rather than busy herself outside of the family home, it would seem that Parsons believed it was the duty, or rather the function, of mothers to inculcate and instil the appropriate societal values and norms within their offspring. Markedly, calls for female emancipation and equality had not occupied Parsons' thoughts for too long, nor had the idea that families could be anything other than heterosexual.

Nonetheless, the socialisation process was not confined to the family and mother alone. Not surprisingly, Parsons went on to argue that schools and colleges also played a significant role in the transmission of the so-called latent functions. In fact, he had come to the opinion (1971, p 101) that, in a modern complex society, it was "the education system, and not kinship, that increasingly determines the distribution of individuals within the ... system". Like with the family, Parsons saw education in terms of its contribution to the social structure as a whole. Not only did education determine distribution, but it also provided the most salient link with the occupational system (Parsons, 1967). Formal education, he maintained, should be regarded as a series of apprenticeships for adult occupational roles. The school system was a microcosm of the adult world where, to a much higher degree than in the family, the child learns in school to adjust to a specific "universalistic-achievement system" (Parsons, 1952, p 240).

Moreover, Parsons continued with his benign optimism when he described the school as being the focal point for the convergence of numerous motivational factors. By accepting the role expectations of the school system (such as the attainment of good marks), the child may become highly interested in the subject matter that he or she is studying. Alternatively, contemplated Parsons, another child could be pursuing the favourable attitude of the teacher or it might be that a child found inspiration in surpassing their classmates. Either way, these different motivations all converge in the common direction of "striving for marks" (Parsons, 1952, p 240). In sum, Parsons was describing how the children begin to accept the competitive norms and values of a highly stratified society along the lines of the US. Unfortunately, the negative possibility of failure is given little space or time. That, he argued (1952, p 240), is simply "another story".

Putting the possibility of failure to one side, the next stage of the socialisation process occurs in the paid-labour market, or, to be more precise, within the workplace. Here, Parsons tended to stress the importance of occupational roles and the contract of employment (Parsons and Smelser, 1957). Besides exploring the benefits of the contract and occupational roles to the organisation or firm, Parsons also argued that individuals entering into the labour market become acclimatised through a six-stage process of institutionalisation. In his words, it amounts to a transition from the pattern-maintenance system to that of the economy with the movement:

> (1) from the most general socialised motivation to 'generalised performance capacity'; (2) from general performance capacity to 'trained capacity'; (3) from trained capacity to membership in the labour force; (4) from membership in the labour force to employment by a specific firm; (5) from employment to specific job or occupational role assignment; and, finally, (6) from specific occupational role to specific 'task'. (Parsons and Smelser, 1957, p 122)

In less technical terms, this amounts to Parsons stipulating that the individual learns how to gain employment (through qualifications); learns to acquire specific skills required by the employer; and, eventually, learns to perform given tasks economically and efficiently. In so doing, the individual also learns how to work effectively alongside other colleagues.

Naturally, one of Parsons' principal factors to help facilitate this change was the contract of employment and, of course, the payment of wages. In this respect, Parsons argued, income is a source for facilities for the maintenance of the household outside the firm. As such, then, the relationship constitutes the *goal-attainment* (G) aspect "of the contract-of-employment sub-system of his [sic] larger role system" (Parsons and Smelser, 1957, p 114). Clearly, the benevolence behind the thought processes of Parsons is again in evidence. Issues of industrial unrest, exploitative employers and unseemly working conditions are not on the agenda for this somewhat positive assessment of American social relations.

Indeed, this exploration of the institutional roles Parsons assigned to the family (or more specifically to women), formal education and the working environment betrays numerous faults and omissions in Parsons overarching concept of society and how it operates. Yet, despite the added Parsonian degradation of women through their subjugation to the 'functional' duties of familial support and socialisation – and despite the "dismissal of group prejudice, scapegoating, and class conflicts as mere symptoms of 'strain' produced by technological change" (Gerth, 1997, p 673) – other theorists, and much later other political activists, have continued to admire and draw upon Parsons' specific brand of 'objective' theory and his benevolent interpretation of the social world.

The benign hierarchy of the 'American dream'

By way of a contrast, William Buxton (to name but one) saw the AGIL model as being entirely subjective in that it consolidated a desire on behalf of Parsons and, by implication, his future devotees to arm themselves with a "sociology articulating ultimate values to secular society" (Buxton, 1985, p 144). To reiterate once more, Buxton – like this book – believes that Parsons had produced a model of society that was, in essence, the first step in a crusade to consolidate, promote and reinforce a personal yet potentially erroneous impression of a harmoniously transcendent American nation-state.

Certainly, this stance is not without support. One only has to look at the way in which Parsons placed the motivational, and therefore functional, aspects of stratification within the AGIL framework to justify the position taken by Buxton. For instance, Parsons dispassionately argued (1940, p 69) that stratification was a means to provide "differential ranking of human individuals who compose a given social system and their treatment as superior or inferior relative to one another in certain socially important respects". In this scheme of things, it is a ranking that spins on the fundamental axis of ascription (rights of birth or biological hereditary qualities, such as age and sex) versus achievement (personal action, effort, hard work, talent). Consequently, ranking takes place on the basis of moral evaluation resulting in degrees of respect or disapproval. In other words, one's status is designated according to kinship membership (by birth and/or marriage), personal qualities (sex, age, intelligence, strength), achievements, possessions (material and non-material that belong to an individual and are transferable), authority (an "institutionally recognised right to influence the actions of others" [Parsons, 1940, p 76]) and power.

This may well be true, but in the Parsonian ideal, the dominant aspects of stratification were deemed to reflect American society at that time and boil down to questions of occupation first and kinship later. Emphasis, therefore, was placed more in the hands of achievement through the beneficial utilisation of presumed opportunities rather than hereditary birthright. In theory, some would argue that this is a commendable and benign state of affairs. In terms of reality, others would beg to differ. According to Hans Gerth (1997, p 673), Parsons creates an image of a world in which:

> unearned income does not exist; rentier income from land disappears into his [Parsons'] murky conception of a 'reward structure'; and Marx's industrial reserve army as well as the issues, so prominent in the 1930s, of 'technological unemployment' and the 'dole' (another form of unearned income) also vanish in favor of a simple and naive 'liberal theory model' through which the Chamber of Commerce's normative image of capitalism is transformed into a Parsonian ideal type.

Nevertheless, such criticism of Parsons did not deter other functionalists that were to supplement the work and aspirations of their mentor. In 1945, for example, Kingsley Davis and Wilbert E. Moore provided a more simplified foundation for the functionalist understanding of capitalism and the 'American dream'. They proclaimed that stratification was a 'normal' characteristic of modern society and that differentiation was an efficient functional necessity since its universal presence not only reflected, but also reinforced, society's attempts at "placing and motivating individuals in the social structure" (Davis and Moore in Bendix and Lipset, 1967, p 47). Within this scenario, motivation had to operate on two distinct levels. Initially, there would be the need to "instil in the proper individuals the desire to fill certain positions" (p 47). Yet, once these individuals had acquired the aforementioned positions, then it would be necessary to encourage "the desire to perform the duties attached to them" (p 47). The "things" (p 48) that enable an individual to obtain sustenance, comfort and that contribute to humour, diversion, self-respect and ego-expansion, were seen as providing for a system of rewards – in the form of inducements – through which the desire to perform within the social structure can be impressed upon the individual. Since Davis and Moore viewed some positions (namely those in government, administration, education,and so on) as being more important than others, they argued that such rewards should be (and often are) dispensed differentially according to the merits of the position concerned. In this way, social inequality, and therefore stratification, was seen as "an unconsciously evolved device by which societies ensure that the most important positions are conscientiously filled by the most qualified persons" (Davis and Moore in Bendix and Lipset, 1967, p 48).

Expanding upon this rather basic and naive exercise in linear thought, stratification in R.K. Merton's eyes (1968, pp 186-7) reflected the formulation and integration of:

> culturally defined goals ... roughly ordered in some hierarchy value. Involving various degrees of sentiment and significance, the prevailing goals comprise a frame of aspirational reference. They were things worth 'striving for'.

Competition between individuals, companies and nations was thus viewed as serving, almost in a cordial manner, a twofold purpose. On the one hand, satisfaction could be achieved once a goal had been met, whereas on the other, the constant pursuit for 'betterment' afforded for a dynamic of rivalry through which efficiency, wealth and higher standards of living could be accomplished within and throughout society.

When addressing the problem of non-functions or dysfunctions, such as high unemployment, poverty and crime, Merton (1968, p 188) saw these as an expression of disequilibrium caused by "a disassociation between culturally prescribed aspirations and socially structured avenues for realising these aspirations". Consequently, the government – Merton's political machine – was seen as having to fulfil "the basic function of providing avenues of social mobility for the otherwise disadvantaged" (1968, p 131). Disequilibrium, and therefore dysfunctionality, was thus depicted as a symptom of functional (as opposed to systemic) failure – an inconvenient hiccup, as it were. Rectification merely became a matter of governmental provision. In this instance, to question the basic structure of society was not part of the schema. The existing structures and relations of capital that survived over generations were taken as absolute. Their durability had been taken as a mark of success and, accordingly, they were deemed to be the most effective and efficient means for human liaison and collaboration within any societal framework.

Commensurate with this scenario, 'opportunity' allowed for the pursuit of aspirational 'needs' and, as such, became Merton's nexus of society. It provided the continuity and coherence necessary for a social structure to survive and perpetuate its existence. As a consequence, the availability of 'opportunity' was the epitome of the aforementioned 'American dream'. In sum, it constituted a conception of stratification that completed the Parsonian form of structural-functionalism that this book is basing many of its premises upon. Effectively, Parsons' AGIL model could only operate in correlation with a benignly stratified, meritocratic hierarchy that would minimise social disruption by satiating individuals as they grasped the available opportunities and climbed up the 'social ladder' in pursuit of their numerous financial and/or motivational rewards. In turn, the economy and society as a whole would benefit as these responsible, hard-working individuals contributed to an increase in productivity that inevitably, in the view of many structural-functionalists, would result in the betterment of society in general. Wealth would be created, but wealth would be fairly distributed down the hierarchical chain according to merit and endeavour.

Unintelligible accounts of conflict, change and individual difference

From the comments made so far, it is clear that this 'grand theory', as Mills (1959) would have it, is not beyond substantial criticism. In his now famous (if not infamous) book, *The sociological imagination* (1959), Mills is scathing about Parsons' over-complicated and elaborate use of language. Indeed, the snippets given within this chapter alone amply substantiate Mills' grievance. On numerous occasions, Mills reproduces elongated extracts of Parsons' *The social system* (1952) only to reduce them into two or three simple sentences. Without going into too much detail, Mills (1959, p 27) argues that the style and manner of Parsons raises the 'sore point' of 'intelligibility'. Consequently a variety of responses have been elicited from social scientists. As this chapter has shown, some see the theories promoted by Parsons as representing either a 'wondrous maze' or a historical breakthrough in social understanding. For others, they are virtually incomprehensible and represent "a clumsy piece of irrelevant ponderosity" that suggest "the emperor has no clothes" (Mills, 1959, p 26). To adapt an old metaphor used in a similar context, Mills was asking why Parsons could not call a spade a spade rather than, say, "a determinate implement in the ... agricultural production process" (Reiss, 1997, p 1). In total, concludes Mills (1959, p 31), it should be realistically possible to "translate the 555 pages of *The Social System* into about 150 pages of straightforward English".

On a more detailed front, however, there is little doubt this chapter has demonstrated Parsons' benignity of thought. Mills also questioned this approach. Of primary significance for Mills was the assumption in these 'grand theories' that the 'social system', once established, was intrinsically harmonious. In the words of Mills (1959, 42-3), the given conception of normative order was inherently linked to a harmony of interests whereby the "'collective behaviour' of terrorised masses and excited mobs, crowds and movements ... find no place in the normatively created social structures of grand theorists". How can it be plausible, asked Mills (1959, p 43), for the structural-functionalists to analyse the US in terms of the 'dominant value system' without accounting for "the known statistics of life-chances based on levels of property and income"?

In a similar vein, Clarke (1991, p 302) pondered whether or not the 'grand theory' approach could decide if social conflict was the result of a lack of integration between particular social subsystems, "or whether it [was] the result of a failure of socialisation and social control?" Furthermore, how does structural-functionalism account for socialism? How can the likes of Parsons and, by implication, Merton account for the conflict between the civil and political values of equality, justice and freedom and the realities of economic exploitation? Surely it cannot be purely a matter of dysfunctionality or merely the case that socialism represents some form of "personality disorder" (Clarke, 1991, p 302)?

In raising these enquiries, Clarke was expressing the view that structural-functionalism was incapable of explaining such contradictory phenomena. As with Mills (1959, pp 42-4) before him, Clarke's main concern related to the tautology surrounding the concept of social equilibrium. He recognised that the Parsonian belief in equilibrium being achieved through the adaptation of the various subsystems rested upon self-effacing assumptions about the legitimated power of the state. Essentially, the structural-functionalist position rested on the belief that where there was a lack of subsystem adaptation to change, the appropriate response to any resultant social conflict would be social reform. Even so, the agency held responsible for the determination and implementation of this reform was that of the democratic state. And, as mentioned earlier in this chapter, the legitimacy for the state derived, for Parsons and his followers, within a formally democratic and pluralistic political system. In short, this interpretation made the state the foundation for its own legitimacy (Clarke, 1991); hence the circularity and debasement of the argument.

Ironically, in the respect that the structural-functionalists actively promoted the virtues of laissez-faire capitalism, this stance violated the fundamental principles of liberalism in that freedom, liberty and, more importantly, individual action were being subsumed by the functional need to resolve the problem of order. Yet, regardless of the structural-functionalist propensity to attribute benign roles and functions to familial members, institutions and organisations, and regardless of the inability of structural-functionalism to adequately discuss the problems of power, exploitation and conflict, many of the founding principles behind such strains of thought persisted. In this respect, this persistence provided the platform for organisational theorists to develop their more particularistic form of structural-functionalism into highly influential contemporary accounts of community and social relations. For this reason, Chapter Three of this book moves on to discuss the origins of the philosophy behind the resultant new communitarian movement and the influence of Amitai Etzioni and, to a lesser extent, that of Philip Selznick. Ultimately, it provides the tools for this book to secure the bridge that links the social policies of New Labour to that of structural-functionalism of the Parsonian kind.

THREE

From organisational theory to the new communitarian movement of Amitai Etzioni

Etzioni and New Labour

Having established a working definition of functionalism in Chapter Two, it is now possible to trace the impact of such trains of thought upon the highly influential ideas of the new communitarian movement of today. It is one of the contentions of this chapter that communitarian interpretations of society have been heavily affected by functionalist concepts and methodology. As will become clear later in this book, this is of critical concern for New Labour in that the teachings, understandings and messages emanating from the new communitarian movement have had, and still have, a great sway upon the political outlook of Tony Blair and his party. Consequently, a deeper knowledge of the theoretical leanings that lay behind the communitarianism of today will not only enhance an understanding of the policies of New Labour, but also strengthen the claim that New Labour has adopted a functionalist outlook in its attempts to implement welfare reform.

The importance of Amitai Etzioni in relation to New Labour should not be underestimated. Indeed, Chapter Six of this book will underline the point more thoroughly. For the time being, however, it is suffice to say that there is little argument over Etzioni's influence upon the new communitarian movement. Ruth Levitas (1998), for example, points to the indicative emphasis Etzioni places upon the 'family' as well as upon 'community'. On another level, Finn Bowring (1997) draws upon Etzioni's calls for the revival of individual responsibility and social morality as a means to create social cohesion. Both recognise that it is precisely this focus upon family, community, social discipline, obligation and responsibility and not the blanket bestowal of rights that lay at the core of new communitarianism and its growing reputation.

Nevertheless, what has not been commonly recognised – and what has not been fully explored – is from where Amitai Etzioni actually drew his inspiration. How did he arrive at such an influential social philosophy, and what factors affected its formulation? Through a comparison of Etzioni's later works with those of earlier times, it will become evident in this chapter that Etzioni has not said anything new or innovative. Neither has he provided a social prescription that actually traverses the old political and socioeconomic boundaries. More to the point, it will be possible to show how Etzioni has continued to reiterate the thoughts and impressions he had gained from his functionalist days as an organisational theorist during the 1950s and 1960s, the only difference being that the earlier micro-theories of organisations have been transposed to fit a macro-theory about the perceived ills and remedies pertinent to contemporary 'mainstream' society.

Although it has been pointed out before that organisational theorists fundamentally restrict themselves to the search for efficiency within the confines of North American relations of capital (Allen, 1975), it is not a charge that has been rigorously applied to Amitai Etzioni, least of all to *The spirit of community* (1995) and *The new golden rule* (1997). With a deeper analysis of the specific methodology applied, it is again possible to reveal the reliance Etzioni puts on his sociological origins and thus expose the underlying limitations of his societal projections. Moreover, it will become apparent that this form of methodological analysis is used to substantiate an argument for the promotion of a normative society remarkably reminiscent of an idealised vision of the US in the 1950s.

Finally, this chapter will discuss the ramifications of Etzioni's approach. Without doubt, such theoretical and methodological limitations have severe implications for the direction of this book. On one side of the coin, this chapter will demonstrate how these limitations are bound to affect the efficacy and applicability of the communitarian ideal. On the other, Chapter Six will investigate how these limitations could well affect the policies of New Labour by virtue of the general assertion that New Labour is influenced by Etzioni's deliberations.

The 'ideal' of American society in the 1950s

When introducing *The essential communitarian reader* (1998), Etzioni succinctly defines the modern communitarian movement as he understands it. He is at pains to distinguish the new communitarians from the communitarianism of the 19th century by distancing his position from the old blinkered "stress upon the significance of social forces, of community, of social bonds" (Etzioni, 1998, p x) and of the elements that individualistic theory neglected. Instead, he argues, new communitarians concern themselves with "the balance between social forces and the person, between community and autonomy, between the common good and liberty, between individual rights and social responsibilities" (1998, p x). Elsewhere, Etzioni (1997, p xviii) sees himself – and, for that matter, this new form of communitarianism – as a responsive harbinger of social equilibrium locked in a quest to revitalise society through a unique blending of some elements in "tradition (order based on virtues) with elements of modernity (well protected autonomy)". All of which represent a declaration of Etzioni's sociological viewpoints and methodology. All deeply reflect his attitude towards modern society and the achievement of a communitarian alternative. Consequently, Amitai Etzioni's vision of a communitarian society is heavily predicated upon what he sees as having gone wrong with present-day social relations. To this end, Etzioni has produced two seminal works to outline the situation. The first, *The spirit of community* (1995), is ostensibly a campaigning book for the communitarian movement in the US, whereas the second, *The new golden rule* (1997), is "more analytical, engaging to some extent with the related academic literature, and claiming legitimacy from social science" (Levitas, 1998, p 90). Nevertheless, in the pursuit of a clear unequivocal understanding of the new communitarian position, it is the latter work that provides a more detailed and contextualised account of Etzioni's overarching argument.

As a starting point for *The new golden rule*, Etzioni uses 1950s' America as a 'baseline' template of reference. He talks of this decade as a social ideal in many respects. Core values, he argues (1997, p 61), "were relatively widely shared and strongly endorsed" and so helped to promote a situation where members "of society had a strong sense of duty to their families, communities and society" as a whole. Morality and order during this period were seen by Etzioni to generate stable relations. Christianity was the dominant and guiding religion. Violent crime, drug abuse, alcoholism and incidences of illegitimacy were low, or at least discretely concealed. The law made divorce difficult, abortion illegal throughout the US, and "the roles of men and women were relatively clearly delineated" (Etzioni, 1997, p 61). Men were supposed to be the providers, women the dutiful 'carers', whereas promiscuous women were regarded as 'sluts' and unmarried women were stigmatised as spinsters (1997, p 62).

Despite a passing acknowledgement that women and ethnic minorities were treated as second-class citizens (1997, p 63), Etzioni enthuses over this past society. In his eyes, low autonomy for certain groupings is not always a bad thing. To this end, Etzioni (1997, p 63) ambiguously comments upon, but is not overly critical of, the fact that college students of the time were expected to take a fair number of 'prescribed' courses which "reflected unabashedly (and often with little self-awareness) the dominant set of values". Granted, Etzioni concedes that American society of this yesteryear was characterised by a high level of coercion; nonetheless, he still commends the fact that it was offset with a similarly high presence of moral suasion. Coercion, for Etzioni, is necessary at times but can be overly repressive and destructive if it is too readily and too generously applied. On the other hand, the presence and pervasion of moral suasion is one of his basic foundations for determining social order. An effective balance between the two, therefore, is an integral aspect of Etzioni's communitarian thinking and it is precisely this detection of moral suasion, alongside elements of coercion, which allows him to use 1950s' America as a comparative measure of social stability.

Disparaging the promiscuous 1960s and the instrumental 1980s

In short, Amitai Etzioni appears to affectionately embrace many aspects of the ordered way in which American society was conducted in the 1950s. By way of a contrast, Etzioni's depiction of events in America from the 1960s to the end of the 1980s tend to paint a very tainted picture which allows him to hark back to what he sees as the positive values of times gone by. Quite simply, "[i]f the hallmark of the 1950s was a strong sense of obligation, from 1960 to 1990 there was a rising sense of entitlement and a growing tendency to shirk social responsibilities" (Etzioni, 1997, p 65). Increasingly, Etzioni (1997, p 65) claims to have witnessed the rise in a counterculture of individualism and instrumental reasoning that "provided a normative seal of approval to a focus on the self rather than on responsibilities to the community". For him, it was a self-interest that was soon to become an unacceptable, if not distasteful, base for social disorder and misplaced virtues, a base from which society would be riven by competition over individual entitlements arising out of an increased political obsession with 'rights' at the expense of 'responsibilities'.

When tracing this later period of destructive change in social values, Etzioni (1997, p 65) declares that with the rise in promiscuity from the 1960s onwards, the role and influence of religion had declined, divorce and abortion were eventually legalised and notions of what constituted a family had been redefined to accommodate "a wider variety of households". The period also saw a concomitant weakening of the respect for authority. No longer, he maintains, was there a confidence in, or passive acceptance of, the actions of those empowered to lead. In fact, the exact opposite had become the norm. Voter turnout had decreased, feelings of alienation were on the increase and over the years Americans had, in Etzioni's words (1997, p 66), "become a tribe that savages and consumes its leaders".

On the socioeconomic front, Etzioni restricts his attention to the tensions and conflicts that arose from the rising demands for autonomy, the unintended consequence of dependency, and the increased individuation of society. Central to Etzioni's argument is the belief that, during this period, "changes in socioeconomic conditions contributed both to enhancing autonomy – and dependency, and hence the loss of autonomy" (1997, p 67). Noticeably, this is a rather circular argument. Primarily, it is an assertion that rests upon the belief that socioeconomic policy had not only improved the living conditions of the disadvantaged but had also created a dependency upon governmental support. By way of substantiation, Etzioni cites the fact that unemployment from 1960 to 1990 had increased fivefold to 4.2 million. All the same, Etzioni has some commendable reservations. To his credit, he makes it clear that the lack of reliable scientific evidence makes it difficult to gauge the extent to which improved socioeconomic conditions had either made welfare recipients more independent or, alternatively, more psychologically dependent. In essence, it is purely a matter of ideological preference. Nevertheless, his basic assumption that dependency rose is evident through the very fact that he introduced the proposition in the first place.

With regards to those in work, Etzioni is less reserved in his arguments. Household income, he informs us, was on the increase. But this was less to do with an increase in real income for the individual; rather, it was down to a greater financial need or reliance upon more than one member of a household having to participate in the labour market. For Etzioni (1997, p 67):

> [this] development had strong autonomy-reducing effects as more and more members of the family felt they were forced to work outside the household and had severely limited time for other purposes, including family, community, and volunteer action.

Accordingly, the family (that is, the first institution of Etzioni's social chain) is seen to be the primary unit to suffer from such divisive trends. For instance, the proportion of nuclear families (married couples with at least one child) had declined from 42% in 1960 to 26% in 1990. Over the same period, the rate of divorce doubled, with nearly half of all marriages ending in divorce while rates of illegitimacy rose sharply "from 21.6 per 1000 births in 1960 to 41.8 in 1989" (Etzioni, 1997, p 68). All of which, so the argument goes, reflect the gradual erosion-cum-disintegration of the moral order within society. Furthermore, all represent an increase in differentiation and help perpetuate a further rejection of normative values.

At the same time, Etzioni remarks upon the greater diversity and fragmentation throughout American society as a whole. The percentage of non-white and Hispanic Americans, for example, had more than doubled and the "percentage of the population that is foreign born increased from 5.4 percent in 1960 to 7.9 percent in 1990" (1997, p 68). Likewise, men and women had become separate, distinctive groups that have grown apart as opposed to forming the 1950s' idyll of two "human halves linked together in that basic human wholeness, the natural marital state" (Miller and Novak, 1977, quoted in Etzioni, 1997, p 62).

As before, Etzioni sees this social diversification as a root cause for moral chaos and tension. Traditional gender roles, for one, were cast aside and not adequately replaced, leaving individuals bereft of normative guidance or, at the very least, lacking a consensus as to what was approved and expected from men and women. For another, racial tension was on the increase and race-based urban riots began to erupt. Tension within the Jewish–African American liberal coalition over social change started to mount, while on another front African Americans felt under threat from the continued influx of new immigrants. African Americans resented the special status accorded to the newcomers and so fuelled "conflict with Hispanics and Asian Americans" (Etzioni, 1997, p 68). Clearly for Etzioni, such tensions were beginning to stretch the social fabric that holds society together. They were tensions that not only had helped to bring about a situation where one out of four adults in America were being harassed, intimidated, insulted or assaulted because of prejudice, but also they were tensions that had contributed to the creation of an environment of general mistrust. It was, he adds (1997, p 68), a period during which the proportion of people who felt that 'most people can be trusted' had "declined from 58 percent in 1960 to 37 percent in 1993".

In relation to the period's balance between moral suasion and coercion, Etzioni expresses opinions of equal despondency. He emphatically declares that the 1960s were marked by a simultaneous reduction in both coercive means of social control and the reliance upon moral suasion to bring people into order. Coercion was seen to be reduced with the repeal of sodomy laws; the gradual removal of abortion from the list of acts punishable by the state; the introduction of 'no fault' laws that made divorce even easier; and the diminution of public support for corporal punishment in schools. As for the decline in moral suasion, Etzioni points to the effects of an upsurge in welfare liberal and laissez-faire conservative ideas as they took their respective turns to replace coercive measures. Traditional values lost much of their power. No strong new values arose, while the notion that one should not be judgemental gained currency to the extent that the:

> rise of the counterculture in the 1960s further weakened the country's values of hard work and thrift, as well as compliance with moral codes of conduct, from dress codes to table manners, from established tastes in music to cuisine. (Etzioni, 1997, p 64)

Notwithstanding a partial return to coercive law enforcement and a revival in moral condemnation, the 1980s appeared only worse to Etzioni, not least because the laissez-faire individualist politics of the New Right during that decade had, so the argument continues, encouraged a culture of job insecurity and social greed which only helped to feed the social unrest brewing in the 1960s and 1970s. *In toto*, Etzioni (1997, p 72) sees the end of the 1980s as the culmination of a growing state of "normless anarchy" in American society. In its extreme, it is an anarchy that is epitomised by a lack of moral guidance and has led to increased violent crime in public places:

> movies that romanticise incest, such as *Spanking the Monkey*; the campaign by NAMBLA (the North American Man/ Boy Love Association) to repeal the age of consent for sex, arguing that sex at eight is 'too late'; and to less extreme developments, such as the spread of hard-core pornography and highly offensive sexually violent material on television and in rap songs. (Etzioni, 1997, p 72)

In short, the period was characterised by an unbounded autonomy that was intolerable to Etzioni and his fellow communitarians.

1990s' America and the return to social order

By way of a contrast, Etzioni (1997, p 73) maintains that the 1990s had, at last, begun to curtail the libertarian excesses of the 1980s with a "*curl back*" towards societal stability. Not surprisingly, he sees himself and the new communitarian movement as being instrumental in furthering a moral regeneration designed to restore moral order. Although Etzioni pays homage to the fact that the 1990s have enhanced the autonomy of many American women and minorities, he still believes that autonomy should be curbed even if it is not completely along the lines of America in the 1950s. To this end, he argues (1997, p 73):

> American society requires a functional alternative to traditional virtue: a blend of voluntary order with well-protected yet bounded autonomy.

Exactly how this should be done, however, is not so clear. Nor is it clear as to how, and in what form, this new society will actually materialise.

Even so, Etzioni and the communitarian movement have set themselves a comprehensive set of aims to strive for. They believe that America, and of course other Western societies of similar 'advancement', "can attain a recommitment to moral values – without puritanical excesses" (Etzioni, 1995, p 1). Law and order can be restored without the creation of a police state. The family can be saved without forcing women to stay at home, whereas schools can provide an essential moral education without resorting to methods of indoctrination. Concurrently, a greater inclusion of the private sector alongside an emphasis on the market can enable the individual to become independent of the state and reciprocally contribute to a thriving community (Heron, 2001). When all is said and done, insists Etzioni (2000, p 46), is it not "better for all who seek work and are able to work to be employed than for some to have high salaries and benefits well protected, only to be taxed in order to pay unemployment benefits"? As a consequence, those who follow Etzioni's example firmly believe that people can overcome mutual hostilities and begin to live together in communities since communitarian calls for increased social responsibilities do not demean individual rights. Rather, the opposite is believed to be true: "*strong rights presume strong responsibilities*" (Etzioni, 1995, p 1; emphasis original).

All in all, it is an argument that is underpinned by the belief that a commitment to the community can counter the pursuit of self-interest and unbridled greed. It would not be the case of having to live a life of self-sacrifice, altruism or austerity; more, it would be a life dedicated to the pursuit of "legitimate opportunities and socially constructive expressions of self-interest" (Etzioni, 1995, p 2). In the same vein, these new communitarians hold that powerful interest groups can be restrained without limiting the constitutional right of the individual to lobby and petition those empowered to govern. It is an argument that appears to rearrange "the intellectual-political map" (Etzioni, 1997, p 7) by offering "a third way between anarchic individualism and repressive conformity" (Levitas, 1998, p 90).

But is this really the case, or could it be that this third way is more akin to repressive conformity than Etzioni would care to admit? An examination of the means by which these communitarians hope to achieve this 'brave new world' will go part of the way to providing an answer, an answer that will be further substantiated with a succeeding examination of the techniques and methods used by Etzioni to determine the ailments of modern society.

Reaching the communitarian ideal

To establish the means through which this new communitarian society will evolve, Etzioni re-emphasises the need to amend the existing imbalance within society. Through the use of a rather simplistic and not entirely representative metaphor, Etzioni proceeds to construct a working model upon which to continue his argument. His previously recounted perspective is remarkably summed up with the stipulation that US (and to a lesser extent British) society is like an uneven three-legged stool where the market and government provide two legs longer than the third leg of community and civil society. The solution to this predicament, he argues, is quite straightforward – simply lengthen the third leg through the propagation of a renewed, suitably modernised moral education (Etzioni, 1995c, p 15). With the necessary revival of the highly functional institutions of family, school, neighbourhood and community, this moral education would start with the reassertion of family values and subsequently continue through the support, and reiteration, given during formal education and future life in a vibrant communal atmosphere.

Only in this way, continues Etzioni, can an ethical basis for politics be rediscovered. In so doing, this will either provide, foster or restore to individuals a sense of mutual responsibility. Ultimately, this would result in the creation and perpetuation of a virtuous cycle where the suasion of communities would be seen to "gently chastise those who violate shared moral norms and express approbation for those who abide by them" (Etzioni, 1995, p ix). Moreover, this vision of virtuosity would not confine itself to the sphere of local communities. It would continue to grow and spread nationally or possibly beyond. To underline the point, Etzioni cites the examples of Scotland and Wales. For him, they are two countries that have already managed to embrace the communitarian ethic. They have demonstrated to all and sundry that it is possible to "combine regional identities with society-wide loyalties" (Etzioni, 1995b, p 9). They are Etzioni's proof that new communitarianism is not simply a utopian dream.

Methodological constraints and myopic solutions

Etzioni's brand of communitarianism, despite all of Etzioni's protestations to the contrary, is a highly conservative blueprint for future social relations. Moreover, it is a blueprint "built around caricatures and straw men" (Skoble, 1998, p 44) chosen by Etzioni to construct a highly relativistic argument against errant social configurations and dysfunctional social cohesion. In effect, Etzioni selects polarised extremes in an attempt to substantiate a middle course already predetermined by his own moral sensibilities. Etzioni's positive recognition that America in the 1980s gave individuals more autonomy hardly compensates for his exaggerated insinuations that this very same society was liberally tainted by a growing feeling of mistrust, increased racial tensions, rising street crime, rampant incest (*Spanking the monkey*) and homosexual paedophilia (NAMBLA). As we have seen, the fatalistic inference becomes clear. Unbridled autonomy for humankind leads to a distasteful selfish excess in the extreme.

In opposition to this negative impression of society, Etzioni's description of the US in the 1950s paints a congenial picture more favourable to the palate and conscience. Notions of a strong sense of duty, shared core values, clear delineation of marital roles, respect for authority and racial harmony through a shared allegiance to the nation-state easily overcome the feeling that America in the 1950s may have been overly coercive in its outlook. For the average reader, this latter, more positive image created by Etzioni is a far more preferable state of affairs which, according to Newman and de Zoysa (1997), suggests the stability of a *Gemeinschaft* where feelings of safety, comfort and a sense of belonging emanate out of face-to-face relationships, stable values, freely shared norms, respect for standards and a paucity of deviance. In sum, it is the antithesis of the violent 1980s' *Gesellschaft*[1] image of anxiety, isolation, insecurity and instrumental reasoning (Newman and de Zoysa, 1997, p 623). Without doubt, the deliberate effect of this comparison is to gently coax the reader into a more receptive mood towards the society of 1950s' America.

Having created this impression, it is then easy for Etzioni to appear to build upon (rather than hark back to) the ways of a bygone era without being accused of retrogression. Rather, he is suggesting that the cohesive values of American society in the 1950s have to be rekindled in order to curb the excesses of the 1980s, and so complement the advances made in the directions of liberty and independence. In reality, however, the favourable bias assigned to the past social configuration tends to sway the suggested solutions to perceived social ills back towards the reassertion of the mores and morals so predominant in the 1950s: hence the re-emphasis upon the traditional roles undertaken by family, schooling, community and society. Hence, the attempt to reassert a moral consciousness that is capable of persuading individuals to conform to social norms appropriate to the capitalism of America's past.

As implied earlier, another example of Etzioni's social conservatism is evident in the analytical and theoretical devices he deploys to make his case. They are techniques and understandings that are also linked to 1950s' America. More poignantly, such devices are characteristic of the aforementioned structural-functionalism emerging in America during that period. In this respect, it is of no coincidence that Amitai Etzioni just happened to specialise in the functionalist-based discipline of organisational theory during the 1950s, 1960s and 1970s. Importantly for this book, it was a discipline that firmly embedded itself within the capitalist system through its dedication towards improving organisational efficiency from within. More crucially, it was a discipline that also rested upon the belief that capitalism, as a social system, is the ultimate expression of human collaboration. Questioning its sovereignty, therefore, was definitely not an issue for the practitioners of such a theory (see Allen, 1975).

Apart from the obvious references in his work to social equilibrium, balance, social cohesion, functionality, dysfunctionality and centripetal or centrifugal forces, Etzioni also manages to apply well-worn organisational models to his examination of society today. In *The new golden rule* (1997, p 13), Etzioni informs the reader that:

> all forms of social order draw to some extent on coercive
> means (such as police and jails), 'utilitarian' means (economic

incentives generated by public expenditures or subsidies),
and normative means (appeals to values, moral education).

This is not a particularly new or innovative observation; nor are its
assumptions objective. To emphasise the point, one only has to look
back to 1973: in trying to trace a path *Towards a theory of societal guidance*,
Etzioni actually used the same analogy to stipulate that social structures
are more than just patterns of interactions, expectations and symbols.
They are also:

> patterns of allocation of social assets, of the possessions of a
> social unit [which] can be classified analytically as coercive,
> utilitarian, and normative, concerning, respectively, the
> distribution of the capacity to employ means of violence,
> material objects and services, and symbols (especially values).
> (Etzioni, 1973, p 151)

In 1961, Etzioni published *A comparative analysis of complex organisations*,
which also centred around the same analytical triad. In this piece, he
attempted to place various organisations into a coercive–utilitarian–
normative "scheme and to clarify certain problems which emerge
from this classificatory endeavor" (1961, p 26). Organisations, such as
concentration camps, prisons, correctional 'institutions' and so on, were
placed into the coercive category since the use of force "is the major
means of control over lower participants and high alienation
characterises the orientation of most lower participants to the
organisation" (1961, p 27). Business unions, farmers' organisations,
and blue- and white-collar industries were said to typify utilitarian
organisations "in which remuneration is the major means of control
over lower participants" (1961, p 31) and calculative involvement – in
the shape of mild alienation to mild commitment – distinguishes the
orientation of the large majority of these participants. In contrast,
organisations which use normative power as the major source of control
over of its highly committed 'lower' order are typical of religious and
ideological organisations, as well as hospitals, social unions, voluntary
associations, colleges and universities.

This 1961 application of the triad reveals the true character of such
analysis. Consistent with organisational theories, it is a triad that is
specifically designed to measure and define the degree of social control
being exerted in the quest for efficiency and cohesion. In reality, it is
about the exertion of power from above and the effectiveness of the
response it elicits from the supposedly 'lower' participants. By

implication, 'higher' participants must be the ones wielding the power. Exactly who, how or why they are able to do this is not the immediate question; they just are. Power over others, in some form or other is deemed as a necessary prerequisite. Only the type, character and nature of that power are called into question. Nevertheless, it is this process of questioning which indirectly reveals who is deemed best suited to actually wield the power concerned.

Critically, Etzioni's allegiance to the exertion of power, and to the stratified societal structures of hierarchy that allow for the exertion and distribution of it, is not limited to the study of organisations alone. The very notion of moving 'towards a theory of societal guidance' confirms this suspicion. Who, for instance, would be responsible for this guidance? In what form would it take place? Regardless of *The new golden rule*'s later call for open dialogue and the reassertion of a moral voice, the problem of who and how decisions about what is appropriate, right or wrong still remains. Likewise, Etzioni does still not tackle convincingly problems over the preservation of individual freedom. Where can a consensus, which is not tantamount to majority rule, come from? Alternatively, if it is to be a minority voice that is heard, the danger could be that those most articulate would be best placed to determine the values and morals of future society. This, arguably, would fit Etzioni's tripartite model perfectly. In his eyes, it would be an informed exercise of normative power from above.

What is more, Etzioni's use of this analytical triangle is in itself a serious – if not a dangerous – limit to the scope and breadth of any proposed solutions to the perceived moral decay. As we have already seen, it is a model that encourages the use of linear polarisations to explain the intricacies of society. The problems of social order are thus reduced to finding an almost mythical balance between diametrically opposed dualities. As a result, investigation centres around the need to discover the point at which excessively coercive means can be effectively countered by utilitarian and/or normative means, and the point at which extreme utilitarian means may be countered by normative means alone. Therefore, the search for an 'acceptable' equilibrium remains confined within the scope of the three power variants. Unfortunately, this is not a true representation of social reality. Consequently, Etzioni's resultant call for the regeneration of a moral voice to help restore and strengthen his favoured variant of normative power does not offer a:

> satisfactory answer to the disintegration of social bonds in advanced societies, for [his] failure to defend the autonomy

> of individuals produces morality without value, a one-dimensional world in which communities are blessed with a cohesion that is neither chosen, intended, nor lived by the people who produce them. (Bowring, 1997, p 95)

Social order, then, cannot be reduced to simplistic expressions of teleology. One cannot simply detect a normative void and then assume that the missing components can be reinstated or reinvigorated through recognition of their impotency. And even if they could, Norbert Elias (1970b quoted in Arnason, 1987, p 435) would have been quick to point out that norms should "be understood as a superimposed layer of social reality, varying in strength and scope but always partial and derivative". Moreover, Elias firmly believed that these norms should be analysed in terms of *shifting* power balances and power chances since a neglect to do so would deny an understanding into the fundamental question of "how and under what circumstances relationships that are not regulated by norms can be brought under normative control" (Elias, 1970b; in Arnason, 1987, p 435).

In essence, such an analysis is not merely Etzioni's classificatory exercise of deciding which form of power is predominant and which is not. Nor is it a matter of Etzioni's tacit assumption that norms or rules are universally present from the outset. Rather, it is the recognition that such norms and rules emerge out of the social process as a whole. By implication, this also requires a concomitant awareness of the effects and consequences of changing political and socioeconomic conditions in which multifarious human interactions are allowed and able to take place. In other words, norms and rules come and go from within society and cannot simply be applied or removed from without. Only a more 'processual' study of human interaction and social developments over a prolonged period of time would reveal this as opposed to the more 'snapshot' style of contemporary comparative analysis indulged in by Etzioni. In truth, then, the flaws of Etzioni's functional analysis belie the efficacy of the remedy since Etzioni fails to address the possibility that the inherent contradictions within the social system itself may have played an integral part in the demise of normative social cohesion.

As we have observed in Chapter Two of this book, all of this is remarkably reminiscent of the functionalism pioneered by Talcott Parsons. Elias, for one, questions the way in which the Parsonian use of "[t]eleology serves as a substitute for explanation" in that power is described as a "facility for the performance of function in and on behalf of the society as a system" (Elias, 1970a, p 3, quoting Talcott

Parsons). More directly, Hans H. Gerth (1997, p 673), in a 1950s review of Parsons' *The social system*, pointed out that Parsons manages to find all sorts of typological opportunities in his work by:

> constructing typologies that echo the analytical features of Tönnies's distinction between *Gemeinschaft* and *Gesellschaft*, further subdividing each into 'diffuseness vs. specificity,' 'status vs. contract,' 'particularistic vs. universalist,' and so forth.

The similarities with Etzioni's methodology abound, not least in Gerth's conclusion (1997, p 673) that such methods are all very well at a theoretical level, but when Parsons risks touching upon empirical reality, "his points are frequently unconvincing and even mistaken, and his arguments take on an unreal quality".

Selznick's functionalist reinforcement to communitarianism

Nevertheless, this communitarian leaning towards functionalist analysis of society cannot be laid at the feet of Amitai Etzioni alone. Philip Selznick is another prominent new communitarian who, despite his student dalliance with the ideas of Leon Trotsky (Selznick, 1999, p 19), has a renowned affiliation to organisational theory and functionalism. In his memorial lecture for Richard Krygier (1999), Selznick reiterates many of the themes touched upon by Etzioni. Interestingly, he openly admits that this modern form of communitarianism can, at times, be retrogressive and reminiscent in its outlook. Yet at the same time he diametrically contrasts this with an assertion of progress. Communitarianism is, he argues, conservative in that it emphasises personal responsibility yet progressive in the sense of emphasising collective responsibility. It is conservative, he continues, when it says, "Yes, there are important elements of decency at the human level, at the family level, at the personal level that have to be safeguarded" (1999, p 19). But this conservatism can be seen to be forward-looking in that it also provides the platform for a future cultivation of collective judgements aimed at dealing "with poverty, racism, ghettoisation [and] all of the wounding realities of modern life" (1999, p 19).

The functionalist penchant for linear teleology is clear to see. So too is the desire to seek a compromise between polarised dualities. Similarly, old themes of family and responsibility are reiterated once again. On this score, Selznick has in the past provided definitive reasons for their emphasis. In an introductory textbook, *Sociology*, published in 1956, Selznick and his co-author Leonard Broom point to the importance of the family and how it relates to the community, education and personal responsibility. The style and logic of the text may be simplistic but, nonetheless, the theoretical foundations on which they have been grounded remain the same for Selznick today. The same is also true of Etzioni. The family is thus ascribed to be "inevitably concerned with every aspect of society's operation … the family is always in some way a unit through which the economic system, the political system, and the religious system operate" (Broom and Selznick, 1956, p 372). In this respect the family serves at least six main functions in relation to the promotion of societal stability and the preservation of social cohesion. First, the family is seen to be crucial in keeping its and society's members in 'working condition'. It is a unit that is small enough to:

> achieve an effective mutual responsibility for each individual's physical and mental welfare. The assurance of a sense of belonging and provision of a needed response relationship helps *sustain the individual* in his [sic] social participation. (1956, p 372)

Other related functions include population maintenance; the provision of 'custody' for the immature; the provision of an induction into society and, importantly for the likes of Selznick and Etzioni, the basis for social control since in:

> developing his [sic] self-conception the individual cannot escape the revealing judgements of himself that are made in the intimate family situation, even when he is relatively isolated from such criticism outside the family. (1956, p 373)

The family, therefore, is observed to be the main instrument of the socialisation process and, in accordance, represents the first step towards full integration into society. Additionally, this integration is also enhanced by a subsequent intervention from the 'socialising agency' of the school with its peer group interaction (1956, p 107) and the eventual prospect of social mobility gained from the acquisition of an appropriate education (1956, p 542).

All relate, of course, to a basic acceptance of the previously described functionalist vision of a hierarchically stratified society which is benignly suited to cater for life chances and satisfy aspiration through the distribution of status, rewards and incentives. As with Etzioni, it is this theoretical foundation that provides the sustenance for Selznick's subsequent communitarian arguments. In this respect, an examination of Selznick's organisational study of the Tennessee Valley Authority (TVA) in 1949 provides additional substantiation. Outwardly, this was a study of the structure and effectiveness of a prominent agency of localised government. It was an agency that served "as an experiment in the decentralisation of federal functions" (Selznick, 1953, p 26) through its declared ambition to establish managerial autonomy, while simultaneously encouraging "*active participation by the people themselves in the programs of the public enterprise*" (1953, p 28; emphasis original). This represents an important study for this book in that it serves to show how many of the underlying principles already discussed appear in actual pieces of Selznick's empirical work. As such, it reflects a trend that appears to have continued to this day.

In this light, it is significant that Selznick, when remarking upon the overriding sociological directives governing the TVA study, asserts that any study of adaptive social structures has "to be analyzed in structural-functional terms. This means that contemporary and variable behavior is related to a presumptively stable system of needs and mechanisms" (1953, p 252). As a result, attention has to be "focused on the structural conditions which influence behavior" (1953, p 252). On a broader level, this also leads Selznick (1953, p 3) to contend that democracy:

> has to do with means, with tools which define the relation between authority and the individual [as] inescapable tasks demand a choice among available means within a framework of increased government control.

Plainly, there is a characteristic acceptance of the structural forces surrounding the organisation and society at large. Apart from the passing reference to increased government involvement at the time, subsequent attention is purely directed at the ability of the TVA to maintain cohesion and efficiency of operations within itself. Socioeconomic problems, conflicts and contradictions are yet again eliminated from the ensuing discussion.

As we have seen with the work of Etzioni, this approach seriously limits the validity of any evaluation of the agency's performance. More so, given Selznick's concluding remarks (1953, p 221) that the agency, as "an administrative organisation ... cannot abandon the necessity for unity of command and continuity of policy – not only over time but down the hierarchy as well". Selznick, like Etzioni, is guilty of inflicting a personalised, predetermined conception of efficiency and effectiveness upon a supposedly objective analysis. Systems of hierarchy are still deemed to be the ideal form of organisation, whether it is in industry, localised government or society as a whole. Likewise, questions that contest the suitability, or even the compatibility, of the general social conditions surrounding the TVA are given short shrift. From the perspective of Selznick and Etzioni, questions of this kind would only threaten time-established norms and, as such, only constitute a misguided interpretation of social realities. As a consequence, the key to their investigations remains with the quest to find what they conceive as a "utopian, but not utopian" (Etzioni, 1973, p 155) equilibrium within the established relations of capital.

Communitarianism for the professional middle classes

In his later works, such as *The moral commonwealth* (1994), Philip Selznick manages to further substantiate these forebodings over his analytical interpretations of society. In Chapter Nine of Selznick's book, entitled the *Theory of institutions*, he develops the functionalist side of communitarian thinking when discussing the moral significance of socialisation and institutionalisation. Almost as a direct reference to his 1956 introductory text to *Sociology*, Selznick (1994, pp 231-2) explains that socialisation:

> has to do mainly with the transformation of human animals into human persons. The moral relevance of institutionalisation is less apparent but becomes clear when we recall that institutions are intimately associated with the realisation of values. It may be said, indeed, that institutionalisation and socialisation have parallel functions. One lends shape to individuals; the other forms groups and practices.

In what amounts to just over three sentences, Selznick manages to provide the link between the organisational theory that lay behind the TVA study and the structural-functionalist imperative for lifelong human education and induction into an organic social pyramid. With effective institutionalisation comes individual acceptance and allegiance to the established norms and practices of an organisation. With acceptance and allegiance come group or communal associations that, over time, extend beyond organisational perimeters. Ultimately, it is these associations that become the most important contributory factor in the transformation of the organisation into first an institution and then into a community.

To fully explain this process, Selznick depicts an almost benign transition that is bereft of conflict, misdirection and failure. Effectively, it represents a similar stance to that taken by Etzioni in his *Comparative analysis of complex organisations* (1961). Initially, Selznick (1994, p 233) describes a 'pure' organisation as "a special-purpose tool, a rational instrument engineered to do a job, a lean no-nonsense system of consciously coordinated activities". In contrast, an institution is viewed as a product of social adaptation that infuses into the organisation a sense of value that goes "beyond the technical requirements of the task at hand" (1994, p 233). Consequently, Selznick sees an institution as a more discerning form of unity. A unity in which the process of infusion has instilled a sense of flexibility and 'expendability' into the association, or practice, and so enables it to demonstrate a willingness to refashion itself "in response to practical or instrumental demands" (1994, p 234).

By way of an illustration of this flexible responsiveness, Selznick cites the high levels of loyalty that individuals invest in their schools, churches and military units as a concrete manifestation of what he discerns as a two-step process of infusion. The first step of which is described by Selznick as being "foundational and formal" (1994, p 234) and pertains to the suitability of an organisation in its transition towards institutionalisation.

In yet another piece of reasoning reminiscent of the circular logic expressed by Etzioni, Selznick believes the first step to be foundational because the "act of association is itself a quest for 'institutional' solutions to problems of economy and coordination" (1994, p 234). On the other hand, formality – the "long first step towards institutionalisation" (1994, p 234) – appears initially through the recognition that a reliance upon spontaneous interaction, markets and individual contracts has to be superseded with the establishment of a chain of command; explicit goals and rules; and channels of communication. In other words, formality comes with the perceived need for "*designed* modes of social integration [to] overcome the looseness, instability, and limited rationality of ad hoc or contractual arrangements" (1994, p 234).

Beyond this, however, lay the second stage of development. Known by Selznick as a period of 'thick' institutionalisation, this stage represents the creation of an internal dynamic of social reality that comes to supplement – and certainly does not undermine – the formal system. In effect, there is the creation of another, complementary reality that has its own imperatives, incentives and motives that in turn lend an added texture to the organisation in question. In so doing, the normal interactive attitudes, relationships and practices that develop between individuals outside of the original, formally instigated constraints become an integral part of this form of association and, therefore, add to the efficacy and stability of its existence. In short, this is Selznick's *"operative system"* whereby the formal and informal systems become the "focus of institution-building" (1994, p 235).

Selznick explains that this thicker form of institutionalisation comes about in a variety of differing ways. Some could involve an organisation sanctifying or hardening its rules and procedures. Others may entail the establishment of strong, differentiated units of management and delegation with their own vested interests and sources of power; the development of administrative rituals, symbols and ideologies; or "by embedding the organisation in a social environment" (1994, p 235). Despite a lack of detail as to how this latter characteristic or intention can be realised, Selznick moves on to argue that each aspect can allow for the organisation to create its own distinctive and relatively integrated *social* reality. Even so, Selznick does have the foresight to recognise the potential for disunity, or distraction as he prefers to call it. Nonetheless, this is dubiously dismissed with the proviso that an organisation – or rather an institution as it would now have become – would have to facilitate its own mechanisms for self-awareness and self-criticism. In a blind exercise of faith in institutional credibility, honesty and a sense of 'fair play', Selznick concludes (1994, p 236) that for purposes "to be achieved, and values realised, the course of institutionalisation must be monitored and controlled; and this must be done in institutionalised ways".

Despite the warning that past studies on these organisations-cum-would-be institutions has undermined claims that these groupings are purposeful, systematic and disciplined, Selznick continues to maintain that his formula for transition is still valid. Criticisms that the actual goals of these supposedly goal-driven organisations are too vague and too abstract to determine policy are not relevant in the respect that the operative goals can be inferred from practice. Equally, the marketplace idea that organisations are better understood as loose coalitions in which individuals exchange a variety of incentives and are "governed by multiple rationalities and negotiated authority" (1994, p 236) is not seen to detract from the overall argument either. More, it is the case that, for Selznick (1994, p 237), there is:

> no necessary contradiction ... between the goal and market paradigm.... Indeed, what makes institutional design effective is the creation and maintenance of *appropriate* incentives and *appropriate* controls (emphasis in original).

As such, then, an open, natural system of organisation that has adapted through tacit learning is a crucial element in Selznick's portrayal of the development of an institution, not only because it is an important aspect for effective leadership, but also because this openness is a precursor for the establishment of community.

When examining the transition of an institution into a community, Selznick moves on to catalogue the operative process on both an internal and external level. Internally, the quest for an organisation to accommodate a distinctive identity results in a profound shift in the source of integration. Integration "shifts from goals to values, from specific objectives to ways of thinking and deciding" (Selznick, 1994, p 237). In short, there is the creation of a corporate culture that is sustained, maintained and enhanced by a sense of community arising out of person–centred sharing in a common enterprise. However, for the institution to maintain this higher level of initiative and commitment, more attention has to be paid to "fragile incentives, multiple interests, and the dynamics of cooperation and conflict" which, in turn, involves "the transition from *managing* organizations to *governing* communities" (1994, p 237; emphasis original).

Externally, Selznick envisages this institutionalised organisation becoming a 'locus of values' and a 'centre of power' where the surrounding community has both a vested interest and stake in its appropriate conduct and continued existence. Moreover, there are external pressures placed upon the organisation/institution to become an integral (and yet a recognisably autonomous) part of the community at large. Crucially, so the argument goes, institutions that place values in a more central position than goals are the ones most likely to transform their own sense of institutional identity into the ideal of community; more so if they can also multiply their goals to cater for a broad range of interests. Thus, argues Selznick (1994, p 238), the "formula 'organisation→institution→community' applies most clearly ... to schools, universities, hospitals, churches, professional associations, advocacy groups, political parties and government agencies".

All of which appear to be based upon a logical and methodological analysis of social development. All the same, what is apparent in Selznick's elaborations is the fact that the mores and norms that are produced from this version of community formation are based upon values firmly embedded in the competitive ethos of capitalism. As with Etzioni, this results in the same questions over the future of a communitarian society being asked. Thomas C. Langham (1994) queries the implied belief that 'profit enhancement' can bring about a common good if carried out by responsible corporations. If, he maintains (1994, p 141), "we are so enlightened as to be able to achieve such a lofty goal, how do we account for the abuses of the Reagan and Bush years?" Langham also echoes previous reservations laid against Etzioni's analysis. Can, for instance, the communitarian emphasis upon responsibility succeed "in a capitalist world that operates on the basis of rewarding individual striving?" In a like manner, he also asks if there can ever be a place for diversity and pluralism of ideas, or will this new communitarianism result in "a kind of oppression rooted in some unfathomable collective choice – a kind of tyranny of the majority?" (1994, p 141).

Furthermore, it is clear that this unfathomable tyranny relates directly to Etzioni's idealistic arguments. In effect, Selznick has produced yet another (but not dissimilar) functionalist based typology of society. It is an ideal that, for all intent and purpose, is barely distinguishable from Etzionian visions of communitarian society that are characterised by a belief in the 'mutual' enforcement of 'high control', 'high consensus', 'high activation' and 'low alienation'. In essence, Selznick's like-minded methodology has resulted in a depiction of society that emulates Etzioni's (1973) notions of an 'active society'. It is a society that "commands both more effective control and more effective consensus-formation mechanisms since it can rely more heavily on the less alienating kinds of power, especially on the normative one" (Etzioni, 1973, p 155).

For Newman and de Zoysa (1997), this typology has significant overtones. They elaborate upon, and put into focus, the implications of Langham's insights with the argument that such typologies can easily be construed as projections which attempt to address "what Derber has described as 'the communitarianism of the professional middle class' and 'is flawed mainly by [an] inattention to the contribution of the elites to our moral crisis'" (Derber, 1995, quoted in Newman and de Zoysa, 1997, p 629). The 'rot', in their words, starts at the top, since Selznick, Etzioni and other communitarians actively voice "a deep concern with civic order as becoming anomic [but] ultimately they provide scant ammunition with which to challenge the prevailing structural inequalities, which are basically the content of the critique itself" (Newman and de Zoysa, 1997, p 629).

Ignoring the social system

To reiterate, it is clear that the communitarianism of Etzioni and Selznick is severely limited by its structural-functionalist approach. As we have seen, neither of the two commentators attempts to diagnose and prescribe a cure for the problems of the socioeconomic system itself. Rather, the overarching system of capitalism is taken as an immovable social fact that has to be worked within as opposed to being changed. Consequently, any social prescriptions that the two may arrive at strike a remarkably familiar chord. Clearly the work of Talcott Parsons resonates through these communitarian prescriptions. Emphasis upon a hierarchically organised distribution of goals, opportunity, power and rewards would not look amiss in the Parsonian scheme of things. Nor would the stress upon efficiency and a mutual reinforcement of personal and familial responsibility. Likewise, the calls for a communal sense and expression of morality and, finally, for a conscientious approach to hard work and community affairs only serve to underline the point more thoroughly.

Regrettably, there are no concomitant inklings of how these new-found, or rekindled, feelings, opinions or values will become universally held and maintained. All that is given is vague talk of Etzioni's idea of community as a 'community of communities' and Selznick's 'unity of unities' through which a "flourishing community builds upon and is nourished by other unities, notably persons, groups, practices, and institutions" (Selznick, 1998, p 61). Thus the starting point for communitarian society is the existence of community in the first place. Yet, communitarian arguments are premised upon the demise of community; so where, one has to ask, does the initial flourish for the revival of a community come from? In the face of the highly competitive laissez-faire economy, increasing job insecurity, a greater need for social mobility and the resultant polarised inequities, there seems little scope for this cultivation of harmony and a sense of community. In this light, the reality of life within the political-economic climate of the Britain or America of today seriously undermines the communitarian calls for mutually supportive and considerate unities. As a result, those less fortunate than the theorists behind this renovation of modern, Western society may dispute the relevance of such prescriptions.

For these reasons, the failings and misinterpretations of

communitarian analysis have serious implications for the development of welfare in Britain today, not least because of the overriding assertion in this book that the policies of New Labour contain a heavily communitarian outlook that is fundamentally functionalist in its conception and design. Considered in this context, the development of welfare policies premised upon normative solutions that rely on individuals being industrious, sharing, responsible and willing to grasp the supposedly available work opportunities given to them become unfeasible and seriously suspect. All in all, it is a suspicion that Chapter Six investigates further by consolidating the communitarian–functionalist connection and then proceeding to relate the resultant viewpoint directly to specific welfare policies instigated by the incumbent Labour government.

Note

[1] In distinguishing between *Gemeinschaft* and *Gesellschaft*, it is important to note that Ferdinand Tönnies (1855-1936), the originator of such terms, contrasted the private exclusive world of *Gemeinschaft* (community) with what Dwyer (2000a, p 35) describes as a "legalistic conception of association in *Gesellschaft*". For a fuller explanation, see Tönnies (1957).

FOUR

John Macmurray, the Parsonian conflict and the 'forgotten' lessons on community

Tony Blair and the hallowed texts of St John's College

Following Chapter Three, it is apparent that communitarianism, as defined by Etzioni (and to a lesser extent Selznick), is a derivative of 'organisational theory' and, therefore, a descendant of functionalism in the Parsonian sense. Being an early purveyor of communitarian rhetoric is a charge that is often levied at John Macmurray (Rentoul, 1997; Driver and Martell, 1998; Levitas, 1998; Hale, 2002). Accordingly, the intent of this chapter is to explore whether or not this is actually the case. By implication, it is also the purpose of this chapter to discover whether or not Macmurray was a functionalist with an associated benign interpretation of capitalist society.

In relation to this book, Macmurray is important mainly because it is Tony Blair himself who insists upon declaring that he is an avid reader and follower of Macmurray's teachings. On this score alone, the work of Macmurray is worthy of further consideration, especially if Macmurray may have been misunderstood or wrongly applied to policy as a consequence. With regard to this latter exploration, a look at some of the history behind Blair's initial dalliance with Macmurray, and subsequently a discussion of what Macmurray actually had to say in his philosophy, will enable a more informed decision to be made in the concluding chapters of this book.

In 1972, Tony Blair went to St John's College Oxford to study law. During the time spent there, Peter Thompson, an Australian friend and fellow Christian, introduced him to the works of John Macmurray (1891-1976), a Scottish philosopher from Kirkcudbrightshire. According to John Rentoul (1997), Blair was profoundly affected by Macmurray's sentiment and prescience. So much so, that, in 1994, Blair publicly acknowledged the extent of Macmurray's influence: "If you really want to understand what I'm all about", he declared, "you have to take a look at a guy called John Macmurray. It's all there" (*Scotland on Sunday*, 24 July 1994, in Rentoul, 1997, p 42). Later, when writing a forward to Philip Conford's (1996, p 9) book *The personal world: John Macmurray on self and society*, Blair underlined the point. For him, the work of John Macmurray:

> is more accessible, better written, and above all far more relevant than most of what I and many others studied as hallowed texts at university. I also find him immensely modern ... in the sense that he confronted what will be the critical political question of the twenty-first century: the relationship between individual and society.

Notably, this demonstrates a genuine admiration of Macmurray whose thoughts and sentiments attempted to amalgamate Christianity with the politics of 'community' (Wheatcroft, 1996). In keeping with this image, it was no accident that, on 8 June 2000, Tony Blair (in his controversial and much heckled speech to the Women's Institute) made 18 references to 'community' (Levitas, 2000):

> At the heart of my beliefs ... is the idea of community. I don't just mean the local villages, towns and cities in which we live. I mean that our fulfilment as individuals lies in a decent society of others. My argument ... is that the renewal of community is the answer to the challenges of a changing world. (Blair in Levitas, 2000, p 189)

However, the question that needs to be addressed relates to whether Blair has substituted Macmurray's emphases on community with the Parsonian derivatives espoused by Etzioni. Granted, this speech superficially acknowledges a Macmurray-based association of individual fulfilment within a society of others, but does it really emphasise Macmurray's fundamental premise that we "need one another to be ourselves" (Macmurray, 1961, p 211)? Moreover, is Blair aware of Macmurray's belief that this "complete and unlimited dependence is the central and crucial fact of personal existence ... the basic fact of our human condition" (1961, p 211)?

The answers to these questions can only arise out of this chapter's more detailed exposition of Macmurray's philosophical standpoint. Only then can this book begin to evaluate the extent of Macmurray's influence on the policies of New Labour; only then can the input of Etzioni's thoughts be fully measured. By detailing Macmurray's teachings and comparing them with those of both Parsons and Etzioni, this chapter thus makes it possible for Chapter Six to identify and define what may well become known as 'Blair's communitarianisms'.

John Macmurray: the diminishing guru of community

At the heart of Macmurray's social deliberations was his desire to move the academic discipline of philosophy from the egocentric notion of Descartes' cogito – 'I think therefore I am' – to a recognition that humans 'do'. Yes, he argued, humans think; yet it is action, as opposed to just thought, that is primary (McIntosh, 2001; Bevir and O'Brien, 2002). With this in mind, Macmurray (1969, p 38) was vociferous in his attempt to "shift the centre of gravity in philosophical thinking from the theoretical to the practical field". Integral to his argument, was the fundamental belief that human beings are, for all intent and purpose, objective agents bound in practice itself. They are not, as had been depicted by the philosophical traditions of the past, individuals wrapped in the subjective art of 'knowing' (Macmurray, 1932, 1935b, 1961, 1969). As a result, the notion of the 'self as agent' (and not the 'self as subject') compelled Macmurray to advocate the abandonment of traditional individualism or egocentricity. Instead, he declared (1969, p 38), philosophy should "introduce the second person as the necessary correlative of the first, and do our thinking not from the standpoint of the 'I' alone but of the 'you and I'".

By implication, acceptance of this change in emphasis not only reconstitutes reflection as a constituent, although secondary, component (McIntosh, 2001) but also forces one to view human beings in terms of an agency that expresses itself through a conscious ability to act in terms of 'the other'. Unreservedly, such a shift demonstrated Macmurray's belief that self-centred action prevents a relationship from being mutually enjoyed whereas other-centred action provides a true expression of the 'self as agent' in its invitation to others to reciprocate (McIntosh, 2001). Accordingly, Macmurray's prime contention was that the quality of a person, as a person, is determined by "the quality of his [sic] personal relations" (1961, p 95). In short, the main emphasis behind Macmurray's train of thought was to define the ability to act as being predicated upon others. Indeed, it is our interaction with others that enables us to demonstrate our characteristic impulse to communicate (McIntosh, 2001) and learn what is mutually acceptable, right or wrong. Others, argued Macmurray, help us to learn how to morally conduct ourselves. More importantly, interaction helps us to develop an ability to express ourselves, acquire a sense of identity and, finally, to attain a personal sense of worth (Macmurray, 1969).

When continuing this train of thought, Macmurray came to the conclusion that community must be truly synonymous with what it is to be or to become human (Fielding, 2000). On one level, wrote Macmurray (1932, p 180), the unique property of human beings is the ability "to live in others and through others and for others". On another, "it is in communities that people exist as people" (Stern, 2001, p 29). In Macmurray's eyes, community provided "a personal, not an impersonal unity of persons" (1961, p 147) since "the personal is inherently mutual" (1968, p 28) precisely because "a person is always one term in a relation of persons" (1968, p 149). It is through community, then, that human beings can "live spontaneously (that is, from themselves) in terms of the other (that is, for and in and by what is not themselves)" (1932, p 180).

Capitalism, communism or community?

Crucially, Macmurray distinguished between community and modern society. This approach was distinctively different to those of Blair and Etzioni in that the bond of Macmurray's community was the antithesis of the negative, impersonal bond of a so-called 'unity' in a competitive and overtly voracious social configuration. For Macmurray, modern, capitalist society was of the latter variety. It was, and possibly still is, a configuration confined to a sphere of instrumental relationships alone. People enter into relations with each other purely to achieve a particular purpose. They do so to 'get things done'. Engagement with others, therefore, was seen to be conjointly partial and specific: partial in the sense that engagement does not fully draw upon the wide range of attitudes, dispositions and capacities that individuals demonstrate in other circumstances; specific in that what is deemed necessary in an exchange is circumscribed by established roles and norms (Fielding, 2000). Under these conditions, individuals were thus seen to be bound by a 'pragmatic apperception' which gives centrality to the ideas of 'power' and 'law' (Macmurray, 1961). Ultimately, though:

> Economic relations, however direct, do not themselves suffice to establish community between human beings. To these there must be added a mutual recognition of one another as fellows in the sharing of common life. All human community is a structure of direct relations between human

beings. Community cannot be constituted by indirect relations, or defined by them. (Macmurray, 1935a, in Costello, 2002, p 229)

As if to reinforce these distinctions, Macmurray, in his study of 'the relation of Christianity to communism' (1935b, p 159), pointed out that a truly communal society "believes in the value of individual personality". Under these terms, such a society would organise and direct its political, aesthetic and socioeconomic attention towards the preservation, elevation and maintenance of a personal life (lived through others) as the ultimate and determining value. Consequently, it would enquire, first and foremost, into "what are the actual, substantive needs of the members of the community". Once decided, its economic organisation would then "be designed to supply those needs – so many houses, so many pairs of boots, and so forth" (1935b, p 159).

Clearly, Macmurray envisaged the creation of a community-oriented society which would not dictate terms, doctrines and values as this would contradict the very nature of 'enquiry' and its associated implication that investigation elicits a response to its findings. Macmurray's poignant emphasis was that it is the duty of government and society to cater for its citizens and not the other way round. Using Macmurray's predominantly philosophical terminology, this would equate to the 'functional life' of a society being dedicated towards the enhancement and maintenance of a 'personal life' in the community (Macmurray, 1961). Since this 'personal life' involves the treatment of persons as persons, and not merely as objects (McIntosh, 2001), and since the treatment of another person as a person implicitly recognises his or her agency, then this 'functional life' should, theoretically, be geared to serve, uphold and value all individuals and their concomitant choices of action within the community.

In contrast, Macmurray (1935b, p 159) saw that modern society of the capitalist ilk "may profess to believe in the ultimate value of the individual, but its belief is idealist and illusory". It does not organise its social activity in the communal way. Rather, the opposite is true. To illustrate his point, Macmurray pointed to times of stress in which a capitalist society has mass unemployment on its hands. In this instance, argued Macmurray (1935b, p 160), the unemployed are not considered as persons with certain needs. On the contrary, they are regarded as "unwanted material for which there is no present use". The unemployed are seen to have lost their instrumental value and have, as a result, become less worthy of consideration.

Furthermore, when these attitudes are transposed onto the

international stage, this depressing scenario appears to get worse. From Macmurray's perspective, the growing predominance of instrumental reasoning – at the expense of personal relations – has meant that the Western world is now lost in what he characterised as the 'modern dilemma'. No longer, he continued, does humankind possess the warmth and companionship of each other. No longer can modern industrial nations realise the extent of their wealth or even their wealth potential (Macmurray, 1932). Instead, nations (and the Western world in particular) have embedded themselves in a set of emotionally devoid economic arguments that are usurious to say the least. And it is within these relations that the modern dilemma arises. How, for example, can it be possible that millions of inhabitants of wealthy nations are facing starvation through the contemporary fact that many "are all over head and ears in debt, facing financial collapse and bankruptcy" (1932, p 18)?

In Macmurray's eyes, the arguments to justify such predicaments are nonsensical. On the industrial side, he observed, economists argue that these problems rotate around the dual axis of overproduction, on the one hand, and chronic unemployment, on the other. When translated into plain English, wrote Macmurray (1932, p 18), this amounts to nations having "produced such a surplus of goods that [they] cannot supply a large part of [their] population with more than the barest necessities of life". So what do the economists advocate as the solution, asks Macmurray? Stimulate "employment through the restriction of output, or even by the deliberate destruction of our surplus production" (1932, p 18) is the reply.

But what does this mean? According to Macmurray, this amounted to a cure for poverty by destroying the surplus wealth of a nation, a ludicrous and paradoxical cure which intentionally makes the nation poorer through an economic prescription to 'buy less' as a means to counter an excess of wealth in the market. Internationally, this line of reasoning reached its illogical conclusion with the argument that:

> other countries owe us so much that we must take strenuous measures to prevent them paying. If we let them pay we shall be ruined. We must set our faces against 'dumping' ... [against the desire] for foreign producers ... to sell us goods so cheaply that we shall be ruined if we buy them! (Macmurray, 1932, p 19)

Proceeding from this standpoint, Macmurray was subsequently able to return his original premise by declaring that humankind had lost its grip upon reality. Almost in aghast of the credulity and inconsistency behind the arguments of the economists, Macmurray (1932, p 19) proceeded to argue that poverty simply "cannot be the effect of an increase of wealth; nor can bankruptcy be the result of a surplus of goods". For Macmurray, it was plain that humankind in general had misplaced its ideals. All of us, he exclaimed, appear to have lost any sense of value. And with the loss of this sense of value, or faith as Macmurray preferred to put it, "we lose the power of action; we lose the capacity of choice, we lose our grip on reality and so our sanity" (1932, p 20). In sum, Macmurray's argument is unintentionally yet amply summarised by Robert Albritton's contemporary claim that:

> Our age seems increasingly to be one of relativism, cynicism, lack of vision and lack of realistic alternatives. Lack of confidence in our rational capacities has led to timidity when it comes to making knowledge claims. Mainstream economic theory, with its abstract formalism on the one hand and narrow instrumentalism on the other, has not and is not serving us well. (Albritton, 1999, p 3)

From all of this, it is apparent that despite the passing of 70 or more years, some social commentators still demonstrate (whether it be conscious or not) a similar awareness of the quandary that Macmurray envisaged humankind to be in. But what, it has to be asked, was Macmurray's solution to this modern dilemma? Regardless of his empathy for communism – or the Russian experiment as he was fond of calling it (see Costello, 2002) – such a social arrangement was not to be the answer. For Macmurray, the anti-religious communist approach, although preferable to capitalism, was incomplete. In spite of his view that egalitarianism is commendable, Macmurray believed that communism (in its most irreligious form) was only one step away from capitalism. Both, he argued, lack the compassion or ability to fully cherish and value the individual per se. On one side of the debate, capitalism was seen to merely recognise the value of an individual primarily in terms of their worth to an organisation. On the other, however, the profanity of the Russian example only asserted the worthiness of an individual in terms of their "instrumental value to society, and will, therefore, deny in theory the absolute value of the individual" (Macmurray, 1935b, p 160). In effect, communism has only substituted the measure of societal value for that of an organisational value. Consequently, the stage may well be larger but, in reality, the question of and assignment of instrumental worth still remains.

To resolve the situation, Macmurray saw an answer in the fusion of the egalitarian principles of communism with the practices and values of the 'true' essence of Christianity. This did not amount to a salutation to the 'church'; rather, the opposite was true. Macmurray abhorred what he saw as the illusory and materialist nature of the established churches in his day. By contrast, Macmurray related to universalisation of religion based upon recognition of the true nature of human community. Human society, he argued (1935b, p 67), would be best served if it were:

> based neither on the blood–relationships of natural affinity, nor on the organised relationships of political or ecclesiastical groupings, but simply the practical sharing of life between any two individuals on a basis of their common humanity.

Although these sentiments are a little vague and abstract, it is possible, nonetheless, to detect the direction in which Macmurray envisaged human relations should go. Unquestionably, this outlook rejects the primacy of organisational relations. The reference to 'blood-relationships', for instance, expresses a fundamental opposition to hereditary privilege and the devastating problems of racial division and segregation. In their place, Macmurray (1935b, p 67) sought to establish the principles of 'fellowship' and 'love' to promote a "unification of all human beings in a single community irrespective of race, nationality, sex or creed". Overall, Macmurray believed that with the re-establishment of the original Christian teachings of 'love thy neighbour' and their unswerving belief in a natural brother and sisterhood, humankind could avoid the instrumental cooperation of organised activity. The resultant 'fellowship', he argued, would go beyond the confines of any organisation in as much as:

> any unity of fellowship is personal. It is a unity of persons *as persons*; and each member of a fellowship enters it with the whole of himself [sic] and not in respect of a particular interest in which it happens. (Macmurray, 1950, p 71; emphasis original)

Equally, for 'fellowship' to flourish and prosper, two major constitutive principles have to be firmly established. The first is *equality*, for the element of friendship (encapsulated in Macmurray's use of the term 'fellowship') is essentially a relation between equals. This is not to suggest that friendship can only develop between friends who are equally clever, equally strong or equally good. On the contrary, it is a suggestion that goes beyond this limited supposition. What Macmurray meant, was that any two humans can *recognise* and *treat* each other as equal and so be friends. With this recognition, it is then possible to avoid the exclusionary nature of instrumental relations that are primarily premised upon positions of inferiority and superiority. As Macmurray so aptly alluded to in 1950, the recognition of each as being equal immediately avoids the complete lack of friendship behind the master and servant relationship. Moving onto more contemporary situations, it is not hard to see that present-day employer–employee relations are also devoid of friendship. Precisely because of this, it is not hard to see why Macmurray was also concerned to eradicate the conditions through which such relations could develop and thrive.

Equality alone, however, would not be sufficient to promote a real sense of 'fellowship' throughout a community. Consequently, Macmurray's second constitutive principle was that of *freedom*; not in the sense that individuals are set free to do whatever they want regardless of the consequences, but freedom in the sense that a unity of two friends cannot be imposed or maintained by force. On this score, friendship "is entirely, and throughout its whole duration, dependent upon the free activity of the persons concerned" and, like equality, enables "for a complete self-expression and self-revelation which is mutual and unconstrained" (Macmurray, 1950, p 73). Although 'unconstrained', this conception of friendship flies in the face of the negative permutation of freedom as the complete absence of constraint from without. For Macmurray (1932, p 180), friendship reveals the positive nature of freedom in the respect that a life lived in this way represents the purest expression of "our own nature in action".

This interpretation of community – and how such a community is seen by Macmurray to operate and benefit all within – differs somewhat to the constructions already put forward by Parsons and Etzioni in the previous chapters of this book. Even so, to fully appreciate the importance of these disparities, the remainder of this chapter will provide a more detailed exploration of the minutiae behind such explanations. And, as a consequence, this comparative exercise will provide a workable platform from which the final chapters of the book can make a critical and informed judgement about the origins of New Labour's interpretation of capitalism, the community and the family.

Macmurray and Parsons: a contemporary conflict

Macmurray and Parsons lived and worked during the same era. A cursory glance at their biographies confirms the fact. Macmurray lived from 1891 to 1976 whereas Parsons' lifespan lasted from 1902 to 1979. A selective bibliography of the 1930s reveals that Macmurray had published *Freedom in the modern world* (1932), *Philosophy of communism* (1933) and *Creative society: A study of the relation of Christianity to communism* (1935b). Likewise, Parsons had works published in the *Quarterly Journal of Sociology* (1932), *Quarterly Journal of Economics* (1934a, 1934b), *International Journal of Ethics* (1935) and, finally, had completed his famous book *The structure of social action* by 1937. These two eminent social commentators of their time never met. No academic engagement appears to have occurred.

Moreover, as Chapter Two and now this chapter have helped to demonstrate, the contrast between the two is stark. Although each addresses the same social phenomena, they approach them from completely opposite directions. From one side, Parsons looked at organisations, institutions and individuals from the perspective of what role they can play in the continued maintenance and improvement of a cohesive and efficient capitalist social system. Macmurray, on the other hand, was not so benign in his outlook. In direct contrast to Parsons, Macmurray looked at the destructive potential of capitalism itself. To reiterate, Macmurray was not enamoured with life premised on and around the laissez-faire ideal. Regardless of the longevity enjoyed by capitalism, Macmurray did not see market relations as constituting a natural 'state of being' for humankind; rather, the opposite was deemed to be the case. Macmurray was steadfast in the belief that such relations were thoroughly divisive. If capitalism is to flourish, argued Macmurray (1933 in Costello, 2002, p 209), then:

> democracy must go. If democracy is to be made workable, capitalism must go. There is no third course open to us between these two. They are absolute alternatives set for us by the development of history.

Such sentiments could easily be dismissed as outdated and possibly ill conceived if they were left to stand on their own in isolation. One has only to look back to 9 December 1931 and *The Listener* to see that this was not the case. In what he described as a 'relic of barbarism', Macmurray gave a deeper insight into why capitalism and democracy are not compatible. Starting from the vantage point of industrialism,

Macmurray (1931, p 990) pointed out that "industrialism as we know it is competitive" yet competition "has no real connection with industrialism". Although this may have seemed a tad contradictory, the point Macmurray was trying to make was that industrialism was solely about the organisation of humankind for the production of wealth in large quantities. To do this, humankind has to unite. Individuals do not compete for the production of wealth. More the opposite holds true: individuals cooperate. By way of a contrast, individuals do not have an automatic right to, or share in, the product of their labour. Instead they have to compete for a 'slice of the cake', as it were.

Consequently, competition in Macmurray's eyes was simply the absence of any organised plan for the distribution of the wealth such endeavours had produced. And the effect of this competition is to set everyone struggling for as big a share of the products of industry as each can get. Under these circumstances, to be wealthy relates to having more than others and, in so far as wealth is seen as the basis for a good life, wealth translates into having a better chance of living that good life as opposed to those with little or those without. For Macmurray, this directly contravenes the fundamental principles of democracy. Under democratic conditions, he continued (1931, p 990), "we are seeking to give everybody a full chance to live the good life [but] competition works in opposition to our aims", because wealth, in the proper sense, has very little to do with being 'better off' than your neighbour.

Clearly, Parsonian notions of plurality and the situation of 'give and take' discussed in Chapter Two are not part of Macmurray's world. Furthermore, this spirit of competition reverberates throughout all of society. To give but one example of this reverberation, Macmurray turned to the example of education. Industrialism, argued Macmurray, has had the effect of increasing the necessity for educating everyone. In turn, this naturally means that schools have a duty to train children to cope with life in an industrial world. This of course involves, on one level, a general training (such as learning to read and write) that is the same for all, and, on another, a more specialised, technical education necessary for the place the individual is to occupy in their working environment.

However, the downside to this increased importance of training for work is that the competitive edge of industrialism enters into the arena of the school by virtue of the qualifications gained. Nearly all parents know, continued Macmurray, that the kind of living their children will be likely to earn depends upon securing a good position at the start of their working lives. Education is the means by which that good starting position can be secured. Consequently, education becomes "one of the great bargaining weapons ... when the critical time comes for the young man or woman to compete for a good job" (1931, p 991). To compound issues, this demand for competitive qualifications in order to gain a good start in life also increases the demands on the pupils to achieve and do better than their peers. As a result, competition permeates the education system itself. And in so doing, this becomes part of a vicious cycle whereby the true ends of education are not achieved. No longer can the system of education give everybody a better chance. Instead, the effect of competition is to push the standards of work "higher and higher and set children straining their natural abilities to get better and better results" (1931, p 991).

As before, Macmurray had made distinctly different observations to those made by Parsons. If Chapter Two is recalled for a moment, it is obvious that, for Parsons (and naturally his devotees), schools and colleges served the benign role of socialisation: individuals are prepared for working life and the active participation in the maintenance and promotion of the capitalist system. Conflict and strain in the school or college was not part of the agenda. Instead the educational environment was seen by the structural-functionalists to harmoniously provide the opportunities for the young to flourish and thrive. Competition was not seen to be divisive. Instead, it provided the dynamic by which success could be relatively attained by all according to their ability. Each would satisfactorily find their specific level within the hierarchy of the social system.

From Macmurray's standpoint, this interpretation would be completely misleading. Indeed, it should be evident by now that the different approaches taken by both Macmurray and the Parsonian functionalists in general focus upon the vexed question of who or what serves whom. From the Parsonian perspective, it is clear that individuals should perform specific roles to maintain, perpetuate and develop what the early functionalists deemed to be a highly successful and cohesive social system. It is almost as if the social system was given the position of master and the individuals living within it find satisfaction and reward by competitively serving its needs and whims as required.

In Macmurray's scheme of things, this chapter has already shown that the opposite stance was seen and desired. To emphasise the point once again, Macmurray believed that the social system did not constitute a harmonious set of relations. Nor did he view the system as satiating individuals with the provision of a sense of social solidarity attained through 'healthy' competition. Consistently, Macmurray was adamant that the state – and not the individual – had to be the servant. In his inimitable way, Macmurray (1941, p 856) would no doubt have reinforced the observations already made in this chapter with the supplementary proviso that:

> The economic system, and the political system which regulates it have no value in themselves. They are there to play a necessary, but subsidiary, part in the personal life of the community. The state has wealth and power and prestige; but these are worse than valueless unless they are a means to a personal life of rich quality.... A good political and economic system is one which provides as fully as possible for the personal life of its citizens, and for all of them equally.

Visibly, the differences between Parsonian interpretations and those of Macmurray are brought out in these three sentences given in 1941. Unlike the structural-functionalists, it is plain to see that Macmurray was not enamoured with stratification and inequality. Plainly, Macmurray believed the wealth, power and prestige of the state and the capitalist system should not remain within the grasp of the successful few. Equality, or at least equality of treatment, was Macmurray's key to a successful society. On this aspect alone, the differences between Macmurray and the functionalists could not be more conspicuous.

Macmurray and the extended family

With respect to the family, or the 'social unit' as Macmurray put it in the *New Britain Weekly* (1933b), there was also a fundamental disagreement with the Parsonian view of the world. In a similar vein, Macmurray would also have profoundly objected to the writings of Amitai Etzioni outlined in Chapter Three. Almost as a foretaste of the debates today (see Chapter Six of this book for a fuller comparison), Macmurray remarked some 70 years earlier that individualism, for the first time, was becoming the truth. Women were being emancipated. Women were claiming the right 'to live their own lives' and no longer living their life through their husbands and children. The new phenomenon of modern society was the disappearance "of the differentiation of the social functions of the sexes" (Macmurray, 1936, p 132). As a result, he argued, the family showed "distinct signs of breaking up. It was no longer functioning as a social unit" (1933b, p 235).

Astutely, Macmurray vilified the two suggested solutions to the apparent problem of family breakdown. Modern society of that day, he continued, lacked a full appreciation of the issues at hand. On one side of the coin, arguments resembling Etzioni's *Gemeinschaft* interpretations of the US in the 1950s had been put forward to prevent, indirectly or directly, the emancipation and individuation of women in order to preserve the traditional family form. A woman's place, so the solution went, was 'in the home'. For Macmurray, this was deplorable. It represented a solution that was bound up in fascism through the deliberate obstruction of women and the full development of their individuated personalities. In sum, concluded Macmurray, this so-called solution would constitute a far greater crime against humanity than that of slavery, which had, at long last, been abolished from the world that Macmurray inhabited in 1933.

On the other side, there was the argument emanating out of Soviet Russia that the state should become "the responsible unit of society, and so organise ... economic life as to provide the conditions under which women can enjoy equality with men, not merely in name, but in fact and reality" (1933b, p 235). From this perspective, the state would have to involve itself in the provision of equal opportunity and equal pay for all men and women in all branches of economic and professional life. Similarly, special provisions would have to be made by the state for the responsibility of children and in turn, observed Macmurray, this would also entail "the removal of social prejudice against the unmarried mother" (1933b, p 235).

The latter solution, in the mind of Macmurray, was more preferable. This so-called solution did attempt, at least, to find a real concrete answer that would be compatible with the true emancipation of women. However, Macmurray did not see this as being the real answer either. It would only be a transitory resolution of the problem since it would lack the caring essence of an effective 'social unit'. For Macmurray, the state – presumably because of its size and bureaucracy – would be incapable of providing the members of the unit with a comforting feeling of personal intimacy. By contrast, Macmurray's (1936, p 256) proposed solution was the creation of a larger more communal social unit based upon the "free personal choice of equal partners". In truth, it would be a family of increased magnitude – not in the number of children, but in the number of adults it unites and embraces. Indeed, the best way to envisage this, he pontificated (1933b, p 235), would be to think of "two families, consisting of father, mother and children, uniting freely into one".

Nonetheless, Macmurray was acutely aware that this proposal could be deemed to be fanciful and, in reality, may not provide a social unit large enough to cope with a truly individualised world. Even so, the essential point was that Macmurray, as early as the 1930s, believed women should not be subsumed by the functionalist male 'breadwinner' model of the family in the ways that Parsons and to a lesser extent Etzioni would have it. Clearly, and quite rightly, Macmurray viewed women as individuals of equal parity and individuality who should not be confined to – and solely responsible for – the socialising roles of 'homemaking' and 'child-rearing'. Such roles should be evenly shared and distributed within a community of equals and not solely laid at the feet of women by virtue of their gender and the sexually biased attitudes of the 1930s. Taken in this context, Macmurray's way of thinking can, indeed, be said to echo Blair's earlier assertion that Macmurray was "immensely modern" (Blair in Conford, 1996, p 9) in his outlook. Again this not only comes as a flagrant contrast to the functionalist thinking of Parsons, but it is also clearly distinguishable from some of the soon to be discussed views New Labour tend to hold on lone-parenthood (discussed further in Chapter Six of this book).

Macmurray as a communitarian?

The contention that Macmurray had a more realistic appreciation of the family, contemporary society and, of course, capitalism in particular does not absolve Macmurray from criticism. Indeed, a dedicated reading of Macmurray reveals an unswerving, yet potentially presumptuous, belief in the downfall of capitalism and the eventual supremacy of a purely egalitarian society. To date, the opposite appears to be the case, especially with regard to the affinity he had with the aforementioned 'Russian experiment', or the USSR as it was commonly known later. Only the future passage of time can prove Macmurray to be correct, if at all. Other criticisms relate to Macmurray's inability to resolve the tension between the construed profligacy given to the primacy of knowledge of 'oneself' as opposed to an egalitarian acknowledgement of the 'other'. In addition, Macmurray is also accused of having a propensity to portray (if not accept) a:

> multiplicity of meanings given to the 'positive' and 'negative'
> in [his] discussion. These words are given so many functions
> that they become radically equivocal. Their repeated use
> for quite different jobs provides the illusion of far greater

systemic consistency in the over-all position than is revealed
by careful analysis. (Ferré, 1962, p 287)

Without a doubt, such criticisms are forceful and, in many ways, of
pertinent relevance to the works of Macmurray in their entirety. Perhaps
the most serious criticism of Macmurray, however, relates to similar
accusations that have been aimed at Amitai Etzioni in Chapter Three
of this book. As that chapter has shown, Etzioni is guilty of a propensity
to hark back to a bygone age of *Gemeinschaft* epitomised by social
relations in 1950s' America. Although less specific, Macmurray can
also be said to wistfully look back to times gone by. His previously
recounted belief that humankind has lost its sense of 'value' or 'faith'
represented a direct allusion to such 'utopian' images of past
configurations. Likewise, Macmurray's (1935b) fondness for the idea
that Jesus transformed the immaturity of Judaism into a revolutionary
blueprint for social development and self-consciousness also
demonstrated these *Gemeinschaft* tendencies. And because of these bouts
of nostalgia, it is thus possible to point out that the writings of
Macmurray and Etzioni exhibit similar leanings.

Correspondingly, constant references to 'community' by both
protagonists could also be used as a point of convergence between the
two. Similarly, Chapter Six's assertion that New Labour are heavily
influenced by the functionalist offshoot of communitarianism makes
it possible for some commentators, and of course Tony Blair himself,
to argue that Macmurray has had a significant influence on New Labour
by virtue of the Prime Minister's admiration for him. For this book,
though, the similarities end there. On a personal level, for instance, it
is noticeable that Blair and Macmurray differed in their attitude to the
established church. As Wheatcroft (1996) points out, Blair is in the
minority in Britain; that is, he regularly attends church services unlike
97% of the population and the majority of British prime ministers
taken as a whole. Macmurray, on the other hand, gave up attending
the church. This is not to say that he had abandoned religion, as this
was clearly not the case; but because of his experience of, and the
churches participation in, the First World War, he had come to the
conclusion that the established churches (whichever hue or cry) were
hypocritical at best, immoral at worst. In his Swathmore lecture of
1965 (in Costello, 2002, p 89) entitled *Search for reality in religion*,
Macmurray outlined his reasons for this rejection:

When I asked myself, as I did, why I had given up the
churches ... I found for myself and for [others] that we

could no longer believe in their *bona fides*: that they did not mean what they said; so that what they said, even if it were true, had become irrelevant....The difficulties are no longer intellectual or theoretical at all.They are *moral*....

Returning to questions of community, however, McIntosh (2001) provides another essential point of divergence. As if to distance the thoughts of John Macmurray from those of Amitai Etzioni and (as will become more apparent later in Chapter Six) those of Tony Blair, McIntosh poignantly remarks that Macmurray was not a communitarian, since he envisaged a universal community whose norms and values develop through the whole spectrum of interactions entered into by the individuals within. As Macmurray constantly pointed out, a community could not be defined through functional terms relating to a common purpose. For Macmurray (1961, p 157), a community cannot be maintained or even constituted by organisation, "but only by the motives which sustain the personal relations of its members". In his eyes, a community can only be constituted and maintained by mutual affection where each member of the group is in a nexus of positive, active relations of friendship.

In short, to think of society as the group-life of organisations and institutions would be "pitiably false" (1933c, p 329). Pitiably false in the sense that communal relations were seen by Macmurray (1961) to be 'heterocentric' in the respect that, if it were possible to isolate one pair within this personalised community, each would be the centre of interest and attention for the other. Each would be valued by the other and would only care for their self for the sake of the other. To reiterate the claims already made in this chapter, it would be a unity of persons where one's self could only be realised in and through the other. Nevertheless, as the discussions in Chapters Two and Three of this book have shown, this belief in community as an arena for mutuality and the expression of humankind's essential 'species being' is totally rejected by Etzioni and the older functionalist tradition. So too are Macmurray's socialist overtones. Certainly, Etzioni, like the structural-functionalists of old, is not at all critical of the overarching social system of today. Rather, he vociferously embraces capitalism and the free-market. True to his organisational roots, for example, Etzioni positively rejoices in the exertion of 'power', 'suasion' and 'law' on behalf of the majority (Prideaux, 2002, 2004). Only in this way, argues Etzioni, can a community instil a necessary sense of efficiency and social cohesion.

By way of a contrast, Macmurray, as we have seen, actually feared for the future of communities in the midst of a modern capitalist economy. In truth, Macmurray would have overwhelmingly rejected the sense of community envisaged by Etzioni. From Macmurray's perspective, such a concept would be utopian and negligent since modern demands for flexibility and social mobility in the workforce would inevitably result in:

> a continuous breaking of the nexus of direct relations between persons and between a person and his natural environment …the end result can only be the destruction of the family and the production of the 'mass man'. (Macmurray, 1961, in Rentoul, 1997, pp 479-80)

Plainly, a sense of community could not arise out of such divisive trends. Nor, in Macmurray's philosophical thinking, could such division be overcome through Etzioni's calls to reassert a sense of responsibility and obligation through the use of moral 'suasion'.

Indeed, Macmurray actually believed moral 'suasion' to be problematic. Back in 1927, for instance, Macmurray could be said to have forestalled Etzioni's arguments when he first discussed Plato's, and later Rousseau's, conceptualisations of what freedom and moral obligation actually entailed. For Rousseau in particular, argued Macmurray, moral obligation was essentially a social thing. As in Etzionian terms, moral obligation was viewed as the formal responsibility for "every individual to will the good, and to realise the good" (Macmurray, 1927, p 537) of the whole. Yet the good of the whole was not seen as the good of a specific individual or a specific group of associated individuals; instead, it was a good that supposedly included all the other lesser goods systematically organised in order of their relation to each other in terms of a universal purpose. Likewise, the moral end was deemed to constitute an end which takes up all lesser and particular ends and purposes so that they can serve the more general and greater purpose of the good of the community. Consequently, individual obligation represents an "obligation to realise the inclusive and harmonious good of the community" (Macmurray, 1927, p 538) of which each is a member.

However, Macmurray believed this scenario to be an inherently flawed and contradictory state of affairs. Under ideal conditions, continued Macmurray, this 'inclusive' good (as Rousseau would have it) could only be realised and determined by the structure of the community in general and its concomitant norms and values. Taken in this context, the prevalent norms and values would have to represent the concrete embodiment of a common purpose. Only then could the community collectively define for each individual their moral duty without undermining individual freedom and difference. As Macmurray was fond of pointing out, in the modern world such an embodiment tends not to occur. Democracy as we know it today, for example, cherishes the idea of freedom as its goal. Yet in practice the modern world has followed the principle of accumulation. In the economic sphere, this has resulted in capitalism where, for Macmurray, wealth is invested and not expended and is generally used to gain more wealth. On the other hand, in the political field this drive to accumulate indicated to Macmurray that the modern age had seen an increase in political power "as a matter of public policy, so that power achieved is utilised for a further expansion of power" (Macmurray, 1950, p 37).

As a consequence, the notion of social freedom that is encapsulated in the concept of a 'harmonious good' has to remain as a vision that cannot be realised under these conditions. When all is said and done, the accumulation of wealth and power means that the most wealthy and the most powerful within the 'community' would be best placed to have their opinions voiced and heard. By contrast, the poorest and least powerful would not be in such a position. Freedom would thus be subsumed by a moral obligation to adhere to norms and values not necessarily representative of their lifestyle or taste. In short, only a privileged few would be able to "strike out new ways for themselves; and they only at the expense of the multitude of their fellows" (Macmurray, 1950, p 36). As before, division and iniquity would still remain. For Macmurray, this would be an intolerable state of affairs and from this perspective alone, the notion that Macmurray was a communitarian of the Etzionian kind has to be clearly dispelled.

Who killed John Macmurray?

In many instances, it is true to say that some of the idealistic assertions that Macmurray has made within his deliberations has contributed to the dismissal of many of his more insightful observations. So too has the metaphysical nature of many of his thoughts. Notions of living a true and fulfilled life through others appear not to be relevant, let alone entirely realistic, to the life of today. Similarly, the cultivation of 'extended social/family units' hardly seems plausible within the fragmented society of contemporary times. Nonetheless, such accusations would miss the point as to why Macmurray was included in this book. On one level, the philosophical thoughts of Macmurray were included to act as a foil to the functionalist leanings of New Labour. To reiterate, Tony Blair's admiration of Macmurray justifies this inclusion on this basis alone. More importantly, the entirely different interpretations of society set out by Macmurray serve to provide a platform upon which Chapters Six and Seven can give a more detailed demonstration of how New Labour tend to lean towards the impressions of society set out by Parsons, Merton and Etzioni.

In this respect, the final chapters of this book note the completely divergent and contesting interpretations of capitalism set out by the two camps. By implication, a rejection of Macmurray's observations or a misunderstanding of his standpoint could have led New Labour to pursue a prescriptive social policy direction similar to that proposed by Etzioni. By the same token, this rejection of Macmurray allows for Chapter Seven in particular to contemplate on whether or not New Labour may have effectively neglected to account for the destructive machinations of capitalism and the resultant effects upon human agency, behaviour, rationality and morality. In the short term, Chapter Five looks at the pragmatic compatibility of specifically 'right-wing' ideas to the fundamental standpoint of New Labour. Consequently, arguments presented by Charles Murray (1984, 1996a, 1996b) and Lawrence Mead (1986, 1987, 1991) are examined in the light of how they can supplement, reinforce and promote the functionalist interpretations of society already discussed.

FIVE

Norms and the dysfunctional 'underclass': a convenient yet complementary critique from the New Right

Ideas that appeal to different constituencies

When discussing the impact of the New Right's thoughts on the 'underclass' in Britain, Mann and Roseneil (1994) ventured the notion that an idea or discourse could only become successful if it had fully demonstrated a practicable appeal to numerous sections or, as Mann and Roseneil succinctly put it, numerous 'constituencies' within the social community as a whole. Only in this way, they continued, could sufficient momentum be gathered to carry the idea or discourse into the policy arena. By the same token, this book contends that such ideas or discourses also have to be applicable to the 'general domain' (Foucault, 2002) of neo-liberalism's current hegemonic dominance. In this respect, an idea or discourse has to be of pragmatic use to both governments and powerful vested interests (Harrison with Davis, 2001). Importantly from our perspective, this framework of understanding not only allows for the continued prevalence of structural-functionalist interpretations of society but, as we shall see, also provides a limited allowance for certain (if not specific) complementary discourses to thrive and adapt through compromise yet contribute to the general reinforcement and fortification of the overarching stance taken by New Labour.

With this in mind, it is now possible to introduce the ideas and thoughts of Charles Murray (1984, 1996a, 1996b), Lawrence Mead (1986, 1987, 1988, 1991) and David T. Ellwood (1988). All three, it will be argued, have managed to produce accounts of the 'underclass' that satisfy and appeal to New Labour's social protestations. Although such ideas are not strictly functionalist (Murray, for instance, would call himself a libertarian if anything), they do nonetheless provide a more than useful point of reference for New Labour. Murray, probably the most prominent of the three, does not have to declare his allegiance to functionalist theory. His very description of the underclass does that for him. By implication, his description sees the good 'citizens' of this world as having to work hard, be honest and having come from a 'stable' family background. Put simply, they have to follow the functionally prescribed moral norms of society: responsible individuals have to be functional, not dysfunctional. By contrast, it is the work of Mead that not only expounds upon the work of Murray, but also directly relates to the functionality/dysfunctionality hypothesis when talking of the 'underclass'. Finally, Ellwood provides an interesting summary of the debate which in itself contains many useful insights and so helps cement the relevance of these essentially New Right ideas to the functionalist trains of thought espoused by New Labour.

With reference to Chapters Three and Four, it will also become apparent in this chapter that the 'underclass' debate (as it is put forward by these three eminent social commentators) is more than compatible with the communitarian strands that run through many of New Labour's policy manifestations already discussed in this book. Undoubtedly the ideas of Murray, Mead and to a lesser extent those of Ellwood have helped fuel the moral agenda. Just as importantly, their ideas also provide further fortification in the re-moralisation project undertaken by New Labour in Britain today.

Charles Murray and the discovery of an American 'underclass'

The notion of a section of people beyond redemption, without role and making no useful contribution to the lives of the rest of society (Bauman, 1998) is not a new phenomenon. In *The communist manifesto* of 1848, Karl Marx (in McLellan, 1990, p 229) described the *lumpenproletariat* as a "'dangerous class', the social scum, that passively rotting mass thrown off by the lowest layers of old society". Two years later in an 1850 edition of the *Morning Chronicle*, Henry Mayhew (in Murray, 1996a, p 23) talked of the dishonest poor who were:

> distinguished from the civilised man by his repugnance to regular and continuous labour – by his want of providence in laying up a store for the future – by his inability to perceive consequences ever so slightly removed from immediate apprehensions – by his passion for stupefying herbs and roots and, when possible, for intoxicating fermented liquors.

In more recent times, this group came to be seen as members of what is now commonly referred to as the 'underclass'. Strangely, when first using this term in 1964, Gunnar Myrdal was pointing to the dangers of deindustrialisation that he feared would make large sections of the population unemployed and unemployable. This usage was not about personal failing or the rejection of the work ethic. On the contrary, it was about society's failure to maintain employment and "guarantee life according to the work ethic's precepts" (Bauman, 1998, p 68). On the other hand, Ken Auletta (1982) brought the term closer to current interpretations. In his account, the 'underclass' consciously rejects commonly accepted values, as they suffer from behavioural as well as income deficiencies. For all intent and purpose, they were deemed to constitute an aberrant appendage to the rest of society.

By the 1980s, the flamboyant Charles Murray took up the cause. In the prologue to the powerful yet highly polemical *Losing ground* (1984), Murray gave the first clue as to why his views on the so-called 'underclass' would initially come to be influential in the US and then later in Britain. Although *Losing ground* was specifically addressing the American market, his comments (as will become clear later in this chapter) had particular relevance to both sides of the Atlantic. "Within three months of Ronald Reagan's inauguration", he argued (1984, p 7), "the poor were once more at center stage. A budget crisis was upon us, and something had to give".

In an argument that could easily be translated into many Western nations, Murray began his deliberations in 1984 with the declaration that the American War on Poverty during the 1960s had two devastating consequences. On the one hand, he argued, this 'war' had made it more profitable for the poor to behave in the short term in ways that were morally and socially destructive in the long run. On the other, Murray believed that, in trying to provide more for the existing poor, the 1960s had, in reality, created a climate of subsidies where more individuals were 'encouraged' to join (or at least remain within) the ranks of the poor. After 1970, he continued, the rewards and regulations of the Aid to Families with Dependent Children (AFDC) were substantial enough to provide the young, poor and predominantly black sections of American society with 'perverse incentives' to condone illegitimacy; to live off welfare by not participating in the paid labour market; and, once engaged in such a lifestyle, to develop a propensity towards crime.

To fully demonstrate the way in which this lifestyle of welfare dependency arose in the American 'underclass', Murray moved on to introduce the unremarkable but hypothetical couple Harold and Phyllis.

Harold and Phyllis were portrayed as having just graduated from an average public school in an average American city. Neither of them, argued Murray (1984, p 156), was "particularly industrious or indolent, intelligent or dull". They both came from low-income families and neither of them had any particular motivation to go to college; nor did they possess any special vocational skills. Their predicament was made worse by the fact that Phyllis became pregnant during their last year at high school. They decided to have the child together. But should they marry? Should Phyllis claim welfare? Should Harold take a low-paid unattractive job? What would be the rational thing to do? Which course of action makes most sense?

Murray attempted to answer these questions by situating Harold and Phyllis first in the context of the 1960s and then in the 1970s. Due to the reform of AFDC during this decade, Murray argued that Harold and Phyllis would be faced with a different set of incentives in the 1970s to those on offer in the 1960s. Crucially, these different incentives would present themselves to Harold and Phyllis in spite of the similar socioeconomic conditions they may start from. In the 1960s, contended Murray, Harold was faced with the fact that his parents had no money. Neither had Phyllis's parents. Intrinsically, getting Phyllis to support him would seem the most attractive option, but the possibilities of her being able to do so were not promising. If, for instance, Phyllis had the baby she would only qualify for $23 per week in AFDC. Painfully, this would not be enough to support the three of them.

To add to Harold's problems, the pre-reform rules of AFDC in the 1960s not only stipulated that benefits would be prohibited if there was 'a man in the house', but they also insisted that Phyllis would not be allowed to contribute more to the budget. Under the rules, if she obtained a job she would simply lose benefit on a dollar-for-dollar basis. Clearly, then, Phyllis's $23 dollars a week could not "possibly be stretched across two households" (Murray, 1984, p 157). Faced with these difficult circumstances, it was not possible for Phyllis to support Harold. Neither could his parents. For Murray, Harold would have to find a job regardless of whether he stays with Phyllis or not. And the only job he could find, according to Murray's anecdote, was in a dry-cleaning shop for which Harold received the weekly minimum wage of $40. Although this would not provide much in terms of a standard of living, it would, nonetheless, be more than Phyllis's $23 and it would be preferable to the $20 Harold would receive in Unemployment Insurance should he give up the job.

Taken from the perspective of Phyllis, the 1960s would, in the deliberations of Murray, provide her with only three legal options. One would be to support herself (if she put the child up for adoption) or herself and child. Another would be to go on AFDC if she decided to keep the child, while the final option would simply be to marry Harold. All being equal, supporting herself would be the least favourable option. As with Harold, Phyllis could only expect to find menial, minimum-wage employment. Consequently, the AFDC option was worth considering. At least Phyllis would have been able to keep her baby without having to go out to work. On the downside, the disadvantages would be the same as those perceived by Harold. The money was too sparse and she would not be able to live with Harold. This, according to Murray, would not suit Phyllis. Setting up home with Harold – even if it did not entail marrying him, which, at best, would make him legally responsible for the child – was her most sensible choice. In the long term at least, she could avoid the penalties set by the AFDC regulations and get a part-time or full-time job to supplement their income.

By the 1970s, however, things had been significantly altered for the young Harold and Phyllis. Starting from the same basic educational and socioeconomic backgrounds, Harold would be faced with a new AFDC set of options. No longer would Harold object to Phyllis going on welfare. The old obstacles of too little money, the inability to supplement income and the idea of living separately had been removed with subsequent welfare reform. Economically, AFDC and the other packages associated with it in 1970 had become comparable to working.

Phyllis would now get around $50 a week in cash and a supplementary $11 in Food Stamps. Additionally, Phyllis would be eligible for substantial rent subsidies, Medicaid (which could amount to over $250 for a mother and child or substantially more if there is a major illness). In sum, deduced Murray, Phyllis would have, in a typical northern state, the purchasing power of about $134. Compared to 1960, this meant that Phyllis would possess "$23 more than the purchasing power of forty hours of work at a minimum-wage job ten years earlier in 1960" (Murray, 1984, p 159). Finally, Phyllis would be allowed to work. Initially she could keep the first $50 earned and after that her benefits would be reduced by two dollars for every three earned in addition.

With Harold, there was even greater flexibility in 1970 so long as he was not legally responsible for the child. This crucial proviso in the new AFDC legislation meant that his income would not count against Phyllis's eligibility for benefits. As a consequence, he would be free to supplement their income as and when the need required. Moreover, the AFDC objection to the presence of a man in the house of a single woman had been largely made an irrelevance through a Supreme Court ruling. No longer could Phyllis be denied benefits because of Harold's presence. As a result, the old solution of getting married and living off their shared income had become a markedly inferior option. Before deductions for Social Security and taxes, for instance, working a 40-hour week in the dry-cleaning shop would only bring Harold $64. Why, asked Murray, would Harold work 40-hours in a hot, tiresome job when he can simply live with Phyllis and not work yet have more disposable income? Economically, getting married did not make sense.

For Phyllis, the post-reform calculations also leant towards not getting married. Likewise, having an abortion or giving the baby up for adoption would not be a logical option. If Phyllis gave up the child, then she would have to support herself. As in 1960, the only job she could rightly expect would be unattractive, insecure and have a "paycheck no larger than her baby would provide" (Murray, 1984, p 160). With respect to marriage, however, Phyllis would face the added problem of losing her AFDC benefits if Harold had a job. To make matters worse, Harold's minimum wage from the laundry would not produce any more income than what Phyllis could generate through benefit.

In Murray's eyes, the incentive to get married was clearly not there. The penalties for getting married were easily set aside by the more powerful and positive inducement to remain single. Indeed, Murray underlined the point with a pre-stoppages calculation of the economic options available to Harold and Phyllis. If they remained unmarried and Harold had a job, he argued, they could expect a joint income of $270. If they were married and Harold had the same job, the income would be $136. Had Harold remained unemployed, and had he not married Phyllis then they would only be in receipt of $134 (Murray, 1984, p 161). The same would also be true if they decided to get married. Faced with these options, Murray concluded that Phyllis would logically choose to have the baby, live with Harold without getting married and Harold would look for a job to bring in some extra money.

To compound issues, Murray did not envisage the story to end there. Added to this maelstrom of ideas was Murray's belief that the American 'underclass' displayed a propensity towards criminal activities. To explain this, Murray argued that crime rates increased because of an inextricable link between the already discussed changes in welfare; changes in the risks attached to crime; and changes in the educational environment. All, according to Murray (1984, pp 167-8), reinforced each other. Together, "they radically altered the incentive structure" (1984, pp 167-8) facing the members of this 'underclass'. Starting from an economic premise, Murray believed crime occurred when the prospective benefits of committing a crime outweighed the prospective costs to the perpetrator. In short, when risks go down, crime goes up.

Significantly for Murray, the risk of being arrested for burglary and the chances of being imprisoned if caught had seriously declined during the 1960s. "A youth hanging out on a tough urban street corner in 1960", argued Murray (1984, p 169), "was unlikely to know many (if any) people who credibly claim to have gotten away with a string of robberies; in 1970, a youth hanging on the same street corner might easily know several". In an implicit denial of morality, Murray proceeded to argue that when this youth considered his own chances, it would only be natural for him to identify with the successes associated with such a lifestyle.

In addition, Murray also included the added benefits the poor had in relation to the auspices of the law. Accompanying the decline in the risk of arrest and the risk of detainment in the 1960s were substantial changes "in the rules of the game" (1984, p 170). According to Murray, affluent people caught by the police effectively faced the same situation in 1960 as they would in 1970. By contrast, the poor person did not. In 1960, the poor could be 'picked up' more or less on the intuition of the police officer concerned. On detainment, he or she could be questioned without counsel and would be held or posted bail (a considerable economic punishment in itself) until a trial was set. If convicted, a prison sentence was likely. By 1970, continued Murray (1984, p 170), the "poor person had acquired an array of protections and strategems that were formerly denied".

Essentially, the 1970s saw an extension in the practice of equal treatment under the law. For Murray, this was a good thing. However, the downside of this was that this change in the rules of engagement had made crime less risky for the poor, "who were inclined to commit crimes if they thought they could get away with them" (1984, p 170). For juveniles, added Murray, these changes in incentives were particularly dramatic. In Cook County (an area which includes the city of Chicago), for example, the year of 1966 witnessed the commitment of approximately 1,200 juveniles into the Illinois state system of training schools. Yet for the next ten years, even though the rate of juvenile crime in Cook County continued to increase, the number of commitments actually fell. According to Murray (1984, p

170), 1976 observed the paltry commitment of fewer than 400 youths – "a reduction of two-thirds at a time when arrests were soaring".

To make matters worse, persisted Murray (1984, p 171), delinquency among the young was accompanied by either the sealing of juvenile court records, the tightening of existing restrictions to the access of records or, as was the case in 16 states by 1974, the destruction of "the physical evidence that the youth had ever been in trouble with the courts". Although the honourable purpose of such acts were to ensure that youths who had acquired a record as a juvenile would not be held responsible or accountable for it for the rest of their lives, the adverse effect of this purging of records was to provide greater incentives to commit delinquent acts. By promising to make the record secret, or even destroying it, youths (and in particular male youths) were led to believe that no matter what they did as a juvenile, or how often, it would be as if it never happened once they reached their 18th birthday. No longer could it be argued that an effective deterrent was operating upon delinquent youths. In Murray's account, the tight restrictions placed upon the access to juvenile arrests and court records had the radical effect of limiting any liability for the reprehensible behaviour of delinquent youths. In short, a "teenager engaged in such behaviour (or contemplating doing so) could quite reasonably ignore his parents' lectures about the costs of getting a police record" (Murray, 1984, p 171).

In addition, Murray also believed that the educational environment did little to dispel this downward spiral. Persuading youngsters to work hard with the promise of intangible long-deferred rewards was, he argued, as tough in 1960 as it was in 1970. However, when it came to examining children with average or below-average IQs in a large urban school, Murray (1984, p 172) discovered that "more students seemed to learn to read and write and calculate in 1960 than in 1970". On closer inspection, Murray attributed the cause to the lack of sanctions being deployed within the classroom. In 1960, he maintained, order could be kept and students could be made to do the work by holding the student back, enforcing in-school disciplinary measures, or through suspension even expulsion. By "the 1970s, use of all these sanctions had been sharply circumscribed" (1984, p 173).

To compound issues, incidences of student disorders had risen dramatically over the same period. From 1950 to 1964, observed Murray, disorders were proportionately so low that they were hardly worth mentioning. In contrast, 1964 to around 1971 witnessed an explosion in disorders because of the 'chaotic nature' of the times and because America began to permit such disorder. Crucially for Murray, these disorders were permitted as a direct consequence of the Supreme Court's Gault v. Arizona decision of 1967. The resultant effect of this decision was that due process was required for suspension whereas the circumstances relating to general discipline in school were seriously restricted. Moreover, teachers and administrators "became vulnerable to lawsuits or professional setbacks for using the discretion that had been taken for granted in 1960" (Murray, 1984, p 173). Faced with this situation, urban schools gave up the practice of making a failing student repeat a grade. Students in 1970 were thus much freer not to learn, and freer to disrupt. There was little a teacher could do to stem the tide.

In the face of this new climate, Murray (1984, p 175) came to the conclusion that:

> All the changes in incentives pointed in the same direction. It was easier to get along without a job. It was easier for a man to have a baby without being responsible for it, for a woman to have a baby without having a husband. It was easier to get away with crime. Because it was easier for others to get away with crime, it was easier to get drugs [and] to support a drug habit. Because it was easier to get along without a job it was easier to ignore education [and] easier to walk away from a job.

In the end, Murray saw all of these changes in incentives as constituting negative social traps. The changes in incentives had interacted to produce a different short-term rationality where satisfaction and reward was geared to the pursuit of the incentives offered by welfare. Indeed, once an individual had embarked upon such a course they would become stuck within a self-fulfilling prophecy of long-term disaster. The trap, of course, does not remain with that generation alone. Illegitimate children, such as those born to hypothetical Phyllis, would face the same incentives/disincentives. For Murray, the problem would thus be intergenerational and would tend to grow if welfare inducements continued to be given. As Murray was to make clear after 1984, the term 'underclass' did not, in his view, "refer to a degree of poverty, but to a type of poverty" (1996a, p 23).

Murray crosses the Atlantic

Although *Losing ground* was primarily concerned with the problems of welfare provision in the US, Murray had, nonetheless, laid the foundations for the debate to continue across the Atlantic. Certainly, the economic situation in Britain during the 1980s was not that dissimilar to the US. As early as 1979, for instance, Margaret Thatcher declared public expenditure to be at "the heart of Britain's present difficulties" (Thatcher, 1979, quoted in Timmins, 1996, p 371). As in the US, welfare payments were draining government revenue. By 1988, for example, social security payments in Britain represented the largest single item of public expenditure, accounting for over one third of the total. In the words of John Moore (Secretary of State for Social Security) at the Conservative Party conference of that year, social security expenditure was "more than defence, education, environment, agriculture, and energy put together" (Moore, 1988).

Faced with similar circumstances to those of America, it was obvious that something had to be done to alleviate the problem. But how could cuts in public expenditure be legitimately explained? Withdrawing welfare from the poor, for instance, could hardly be justified if they were not at fault. Arguably, it was Murray's highly controversial portrayal of life in an American 'underclass' that provided the initial justification. Murray's deliberations appeared to provide solutions. His ideas seemed to encapsulate the current thinking of both government and the growing influence of the 'New Right' by pandering "to their underlying belief in individual responsibility and minimum intervention by the state in welfare" (Walker, 1996, p 66).

With the proud, persistent support and sponsorship of *The Sunday Times* and the News International Group (Mann and Roseneil, 1994), Murray – without any sizeable academic following in Britain – provided reinforcement and vindication for an emergent climate of thought. By 1987, meetings with representatives from the Prime Minister's Policy Unit, the Department of Health and Social Security (DHSS) and the Treasury Office, helped to cement his claims at a higher level. Two years later he addressed Prime Minister Thatcher herself (Dean and Taylor-Gooby, 1992; Mann and Roseneil, 1994). Without doubt, Murray was beginning to find a receptive audience. As a result, he was able to successfully promote commentaries that appealed to the growing concerns of the time.

From the outset, Murray played to his new-found British audience with his emotive language and worrying protestations. In his words (1996a, p 25), he arrived in Britain as "a visitor from a plague area come to see whether the disease is spreading". Rises in violent crime, illegitimacy and increases in economic inactivity were again used to detect the presence of a growing 'underclass'. In the late 1980s, when Murray first came to Britain, he declared (1996a, p 33) that property crime in England and Wales was already slightly higher than that in America: reported burglaries in 1988, for instance, stood at 1,623 per 100,000 population in England and Wales, whereas the figure stood at 1,309 in the US. Motor theft showed a similar trend. By the time Murray paid his second visit in 1993, he argued that property crime in England and Wales had jumped 42% while the figure for America remained unchanged. The net result was that the "risk of being burgled in England [was] more than twice that in the United States" (Murray, 1996b, p 99).

Regarding violent crime, the situation was not as bleak in 1988. England and Wales recorded just 624 homicides. In stark contrast, the US recorded 20,675 (Murray, 1996a, p 34). As for violent crime in general, England and Wales had by 1988 only 314 incidents reported per 100,000 people. Worryingly, however, Murray pointed out that the most frequent offenders were males in the second half of their teens. Yet on both sides of the Atlantic, the size of this young male cohort had decreased. In the UK, continued Murray (1996a, pp 34-5), the number of males aged 15-19 hit its peak in 1982 and subsequently decreased "both as a percentage of the population and in raw numbers (by a little more than 11% in both cases)". One would have thought that the violent crime would have decreased because of this. Emphatically, Murray declared it had not. By 1992, the situation was worse. The figure for violent crimes in the UK had risen by a little over 40%, even to the extent that the violent crime rate in England and Wales was the same as that "in the United States in 1985" (Murray, 1996b, p 100).

When turning his attention towards the rise in illegitimacy, Murray highlighted the fact that in 1979 Britain's illegitimacy ratio was 10.6% and reflected one of the lowest rates in the industrialised West. By 1982, the figure shot up to 14.1% while in 1985 it rose to 18.9%. In 1988, the figure had risen to 25.6% (1996a, p 26) only to be surpassed in 1992 when the figure grew to 31.2%. If this trend continued in England and Wales, added Murray (1996b, p 100), "half of all births will be out of wedlock by 2003".

In relation to the third and final 'warning signal' (the indicator of economic inactivity), Murray stipulated that, in the 1981 census, 11.3% of working-aged men in the potential labour force were unemployed, whereas 9.6% of working-aged men were economically inactive altogether. In 1991, the census recorded the figure of 11% as being representative of the working-aged unemployed. This, as Murray rightly observed, was almost identical to the figure for 1981. Conversely, the percentage of working-aged men who were economically inactive had risen significantly to 13.3% (1996b, p 100). In sum, concluded Murray (1996b, p 101), all of these statistics point to the worrying consensus that "something resembling an underclass is growing" in Britain.

Nonetheless, the mere recitation of all these facts and figures, taken on their own, could not offer the reader a comprehensive explanation as to why such trends represented the growth of a problematic 'underclass' in Britain. Consequently, Murray went beyond making the association with the problems in the US and further substantiated his arguments with reference to British case histories similar to those of Harold and Phyllis in *Losing ground*. This time, Murray initially reproduced a conversation he had with 'Scully' who came from what Murray believed to be "the capital of Britain's black economy" (1996b, p 117): Liverpool.

Murray claimed this conversation with Scully to be true and representative. Scully is said to have claimed to be the father of two school-age children, both by the same partner. The partner was in receipt of £80 per week for herself (presumably from social security benefits, but Murray does not make this clear), £80 per month for the children, and she had her housing benefit on top of that. Scully, on the other hand, was receiving £88 per fortnight from income support. Added to all of this, is the arrangement Scully had with his mate who rents a room to Scully. In reality, Scully does not live there. Nevertheless, this "dodge nets Scully another £100 a month after splitting it with his mate" (1996b, p 118). As it stood, all of this added up to £276 in cash for Scully every month, £400 for his partner plus free housing.

To compound issues, Murray added that both Scully and his partner were also given a break on Council Tax. Likewise, their children were entitled to free school meals and free uniforms. Consequently, the total value for Scully and his partner rose substantially. After making allowances for the fact that Scully and his partner were not paying tax on any income received, Murray concluded that all of these schemes would be worth somewhere in the region of £900 and £1,000 per month to this couple from Liverpool. If this was not enough, Scully also had an 'off-the-books' job in Birmingham, "where he spends most of each week, returning to the north at weekends to see the family and to register for the dole" (Murray, 1996b, p 118).

After listening to what Scully was saying, it became painfully obvious to Murray that Scully was in a far better financial position from these illicit undertakings than he would have been had he taken any of the regular full-time jobs that may have been open to him. Again, Murray puts the reason for this form of behaviour down to rationality and logic. For Murray (1996b, p 119), the reality that faces a young man in today's low-skilled, working-class neighbourhoods is a world in which 'fiddling the system' no longer constitutes "a moral black mark against you". Consequently, attitudes in Murray's depiction have shifted. No longer is it a question of individuals abiding by the rules and playing it straight. Rather, it is a question of how much you can get if you cheat the system. In the words of Scully (cited by Murray, 1996b, p 118), the "system is there to be f★★★ed….You're soft if you don't".

To explain the reason for the growth of illegitimacy in Britain, Murray once again reverted to his tried and trusted formula of anecdotal evidence. This time, Murray introduced his readers to Ross and Stacey who were in their late teens. Stacey (like Phyllis earlier in the US) was pregnant. Stacey would prefer to keep the baby. They considered their options. In 1991, Ross had a manual job paying £228 per week, which was "better than most unskilled young men just getting started" (Murray, 1996b, p 120). If Ross and Stacey were married, considered Murray, then they could expect an after-tax income of around £152 per week once family credit and other pertinent benefits had been added in. On the other hand, if they do not get married, then they would have an untaxed amount of £74 per week in benefit for Stacey and the baby plus £142 a week after tax income from Ross as a single unmarried person. In total, Ross and Stacey would be in receipt of a weekly sum of £216 when all deductions have been taken into consideration. In other words, they would be given a weekly 'premium' of £64 per week for not being married (1996b, p 120).

Had Ross not been employed, the incentive for Stacey to marry him would be even less. At least the employed Ross had prospects for the future. Without a job, there would be no attraction as a future provider. He would be worth less as a husband than a live-in lover. To demonstrate the point, Murray stipulated that if one added up the income support and the family premium for a married couple it would come to £94 per week plus a council flat. If they were not to get married, the same benefit package would amount to £108 per week. This would be a difference of £14 and, although little to some, would comprise of "a raise of 15% over the income they would have if they married" (Murray, 1996b, p 120). Furthermore, after the baby is born, Stacey would be able to supplement her income by £15 without affecting her benefits. This would be three times the disregard she would have received had she been married. As for Ross, questioned Murray, why should he take responsibility for the child? It makes no logical sense.

As he had before in America, Murray viewed the problem to be intergenerational. Primarily, he believed that the civilising process could not occur in communities where the two-parent family was not the norm. In Murray's deliberations, the problem of immorality and welfare dependency would almost inevitably continue to be transmitted through successive generations of the 'underclass'. Primarily, the blame was laid squarely at the feet of lone-motherhood. The real problem with this 'alternative' of unmarried parenthood, concluded Murray, was that such an arrangement offers no real alternative for the socialisation of young boys. For males, he maintained (1996b, p 121), "the ethical code of the two-parent family is the only game in town".

Effectively, the basis of Murray's argument was that the 'underclass' was making the rational decision to ignore the orderly norm of the 'work ethic' (Bauman, 1998, pp 83-6). In so doing, they appear to be marginalising *themselves* from the rest of society. Therefore, they had rendered themselves to be inappropriate recipients of welfare aid. Accordingly, the logical solution for Murray was to withdraw welfare from this 'undeserving' poor altogether in a stark contrast to the 'genuine', 'deserving' poor such as the aged, disabled or infirm. With this retraction, closed Murray, this 'underclass' would be encouraged, if not forced, back into the 'working' sectors of society.

Murray and the critics

Like all prominent figures, Murray was not without his critics. In America, attention was soon focused upon the highly controversial *Losing ground*. By 1986, Ellwood and Summers, for example, attempted to redress three main characteristics of an 'underclass' culture. First, they questioned the validity of Murray's assertion that the 'perverse' incentives of welfare had actively encouraged a decrease in labour force participation by young urban black males. A male youth living alone in 1982, they noted, could only expect benefits of $70 per month as opposed to a minimum wage of $450 per month after taxes and expenses. The picture differed little if he had been living at home with his parents. Indeed, to compound issues, if the youth had fathered an illegitimate child there was no automatic guarantee that his 'partner' would be willing to support him as well as the child. With this in mind, Murray's racially oriented prediction that a black single mother would opt to use AFDC to facilitate black male indolence is highly fallacious. Accordingly, it is "extremely unlikely", in the view of Ellwood and Summers (1986, p 75), "that welfare programs have robbed young black men of an incentive to work with their direct effects".

To counter any notion that the behaviour of the 'underclass' could have been the product of generous welfare provision, Ellwood and Summers (1986) turned to the statistics for black youth employment. In 1975, for example, they noticed that 23% of young black males that were living with two parents had jobs. In comparison, 21% of those living with one parent also had jobs. By 1980, 32% of 'out-of-school', inner-city black youth had jobs, whereas the figure was 38% for the black youths living in the suburbs. Similarly, in non-farm rural areas the figure was 35% (1986, p 75). Unquestionably, all of these figures were significantly lower than those for their white equivalents. However, the significance of these statistics lay in the relative uniformity of the figures produced. For Ellwood and Summers, it was clear that the similarity of the results relating to different family and geographical backgrounds suggested that the far wider problem of racial discrimination was the real reason for the lower labour force participation: in other words, it was not simply about Murray's rather shallow belief that welfare policy was the root cause of a breakdown in family values and in the traditional incentives to work.

Finally, with specific regard to Murray's claim that welfare encouraged single parenthood, Ellwood and Summers looked at the percentages of all children living in a female-headed household and compared them to the percentages of children who have received AFDC since 1960. For Murray (1984, pp 126-7), support for the 'underclass' hypothesis could be found in his assertion that 1980 had witnessed a situation in which "48% of live births among blacks were to single women, compared to 17% in 1950 [while] white illegitimate births ... remained ... much lower". By contrast, the investigation undertaken by Ellwood and Summers found that the percentage of all children living in female-headed households since 1972 had, indeed, jumped quite dramatically from 14% to almost 20%. During the same period, the percentage of all children who were in homes collecting AFDC remained constant. Moreover, the figures were even more dramatic when applied to black Americans. Between 1972 and 1980, they discovered, the number of black children in female-headed families rose nearly 20% whereas the "number of black children on AFDC actually *fell* by 5 per cent" (Ellwood and Summers, 1986, p 68).

On this score alone, Murray's accusations simply did not hold up. If, to give Murray credence, AFDC was actually pulling families apart through the encouragement given to live a life within single parent units – or rather units consisting of single mothers – then why, questioned Ellwood and Summers (1986, p 68), would the number of children on the programme overall remain constant during the "period in our history when family structures changed the most"? The inducements simply could not be there. Had they been, a larger number of children on AFDC would have been recorded rather than the numbers remaining constant.

Equally, Murray's belief that there was a sharp rise in the fraction of all births to unmarried black mothers was also deemed to be inaccurate. Yes, Ellwood and Summers agreed, births to single black mothers appeared proportionately higher. But this was only because their fall in the birth rate was only 13% as opposed to the much larger 38% drop for married black women (Ellwood and Summers, 1986, p 69). Thus, a proportionate increase in the births to single mothers was the inevitable consequence of this smaller, sectional decrease in the birth rate overall. At the same time, the birth rate for white, unmarried mothers actually rose by 27%. As a consequence, Ellwood and Summers concluded (1986, p 69), it seems "difficult to argue that AFDC was a major influence in unmarried births when there was simultaneously a rise in the birth rate to unmarried whites and a fall in the rate for unmarried blacks".

In the light of such criticism, it is possible to argue that Murray's interpretation and selection of the evidence was somewhat limited and myopic. Indeed, this lack of appreciation of a broader picture gleaned through 'case' histories and the narrow interpretation of the available statistics also provided fuel for Murray's critics in Britain. On a general level, for example, David (1996, p 150) criticised Murray's propensity to use anecdotal evidence in the "gross form of caricature or stereotyping". On another level, Mann (1992) questioned Murray's logic. If, as Murray insisted, the growth of an 'underclass' was principally attributed to the generous provision of welfare, then why, asked Mann, was an 'underclass' thought to be so large in Victorian England? Was poor relief, he continued (1992, p 107), "so generous in the 1870s and 1880s that it undermined family values, thrift and individual effort"?

In a similarly inquisitive manner, Brown (1996), questioned whether it was possible – over a protracted period of time – to view the underclass as a homogeneous, problematic entity. In this respect, her focus was upon single mothers. Aptly, she pointed to the duration periods that differing categories of lone mothers spent on claiming Supplementary Benefit (SB). Up to 1981, she discovered, 7.8% of single mothers and 9.6% of divorced mothers had claimed SB for more than ten years. For five to nine years, the figures rose to 15.6% and 27.4% respectively. This gave collective figures, for five years or more, amounting to 23.4% and 37%. By 1987, the duration figure for single, never-married mothers had risen to 27%. Yet strikingly, argued Brown (1996, p 62), these figures simply did not support Murray's overarching thesis since single mothers as a group still tended "to spend shorter periods on benefit than divorced mothers, or indeed than widowed mothers".

This stand against Murray's use of statistics was not without support. Walker (1996) discovered that there was a median duration of 35 months of lone-parenthood status for single, never-married women. In contrast, women who became lone parents through marriage breakdown spent a median duration of 59 months (Walker, 1996, p 70). That aside, Walker moved on to cogently argue that Murray failed to give any scientific justification for his selection of the particular indicators used to signify the growing presence of an irresponsible underclass. Why, for instance, would a growth in illegitimacy be symptomatic of an underclass rather than a decline in the importance given to marriage as an institution? Why, also, would an increase in illegitimacy reflect a growth in irresponsible parenthood? As Walker (1996, p 69) pointed out, Murray's proposition neglected to account for changing attitudes and the fact that "the latest official figures show that at least half of the children born outside marriage in 1986 ... had parents who were living together".

Going beyond the issues surrounding lone-motherhood, Dean and Taylor-Gooby (1992) queried Murray's reasons for the increases in economic inactivity. For them (1992, p 11), "far and away the most important reason for the rise in poverty in the 1980s was the enormous increase in the level of unemployment". Industry and manufacturing were on the decline, women were much more attached to the labour force "albeit largely in segments such as part-time employment and the service sector" (Bagguley and Mann, 1992, p 123), and at the height of the recession in the 1980s, school-leavers faced unemployment rates of up to 50% (Walker, 1996, p 69). All seriously affected the labour force participation of males. Yet for Murray to distinguish between the attitudes to work of the young and old was completely erroneous. According to research undertaken among the 'aristocracy' of skilled labour in Sheffield during this period, the fathers of the young people that Murray often criticised were also dismayed "by the sheer hopelessness of their search for work" (Walker, 1996, p 69). Here again, to dismiss non-work as a behavioural characteristic of an 'underclass' and irresponsible young males was simply inaccurate and misleading.

Taken as a collective whole, the British critics concluded that Murray was guilty of 'blaming the victim' (Bagguley and Mann, 1992; Dean and Taylor-Gooby, 1992; Mann, 1992; Walker, 1996) for their predicament rather than examining the possible demographic and socioeconomic circumstances that have impacted upon the poor. In the words of Bagguley and Mann (1992, p 115), the propositions put forward by Murray represented a theoretical viewpoint that marked "a subtle shift ... from the problems faced by the 'underclass' to the problem *of* the 'underclass'". By contrast, Murray was guilty of paying little, if any, attention to the far greater benefits paid to the middle classes through occupational and fiscal forms of welfare (Titmuss, 1958). Such benefits were not, in Murray's mind, deemed to undermine the moral fabric of society. Noticeably, company car drivers, owner-occupiers, members of occupational pension schemes and those in receipt of tax subsidies were not berated for their "sexual immorality, violent nature or illegitimacy rates" (Mann, 1992, p 107).

Lawrence Mead: the more friendly face

Charles Murray, however, was not the only American to have an influence upon the policy debates surrounding the 'underclass'. Certainly, it is true that despite all of the criticisms levelled at Murray and his work, Murray's ideas have still persisted in the welfare debates of both the US and in Britain today. Arguably, this persistence may have been aided and abetted by the intervention of Lawrence Mead. Indeed, Mead is important to this book on three levels. First, the inclusion of Mead provides an insightful understanding of the reasons why such ideas have still maintained credibility in the face of intense and, at times, heated criticism. Second, Mead is important in the respect that he built upon Murray's studies of the 'underclass' and provided politicians and academics with a more acceptable and practical solution to the perceived problem. Third, and finally, Mead provides the link with functionalism and, in so doing, cements the basic premise that the beliefs and ideas of Murray helped to supplement and reinforce the functionalist foundations of the social policies put forward by New Labour.

In respect of Mead's first aspect of importance, one only has to turn to Mead's 1988 review of Murray's *Losing ground* (1984). In his review, Mead (1988, p 23) assertively pointed out that this book marked a "sea change in the style of research and argument about poverty". For Mead, the book was powerfully written, expressed clear thought, could easily be understood by the ordinary reader and was fearless in its assertions and conclusions. Without going over all of the details already discussed, a crucial element of Mead's support for Murray was the recognition that it is true that "the bottom fell out of poor, and especially black, society at the time of the Great Society" (1988, p 25). It was also true, he continued, that the social indicators of illegitimacy, welfarism, crime, school-failure and non-work had turned sharply worse for 'blacks'.

Setting this agreement to one side, however, Mead moved on to enthusiastically argue that the strength of Murray's book lay in its affinity to the venerable Anglo-Saxon tradition of moderate individualism. In Mead's mind (1988, p 26), the book was reminiscent of the "American Founders, Adam Smith and John Locke". Consequently, the theme of the book permeated throughout all of Murray's detailed discussions and, as a direct result, gave *Losing ground* a theoretical vision that was both unified and forceful. By contrast, maintained Mead, so few of Murray's critics came from the philosophical ranks. Rather, they were technicians who specialised in data analysis and data analysis alone. All too often, for Mead, the focus of these technicians was too narrow. In truth, they only demonstrated knowledge of one particular data set (such as the statistics relating to poverty) and the specific disputes that surround it. Even so, Mead did admit that some of the criticisms were well made and well taken. Yet in the end analysis, he deemed them to be ill equipped to successfully challenge Murray's more comprehensive vision. Dismissively, Mead (1988, p 26) believed that "Murray's broad argument trampled on any number of these specialists as it ranged from welfare to employment, to crime and education policy". Clearly, Mead held Murray's work in high regard.

Nonetheless, Mead did have some reservations. In particular, he expressed concern over Murray's loose historical argument and the dubious assumption that crime, illegitimacy or non-work actually served the interests of the poor. Where he and Murray differed most sharply, was in their respective visions of human nature. From Murray's vantage, poor adults are short-sighted, rational calculative individuals tempted by the disincentives of welfare. From Mead's (1991, p 20) point of view, the poor are depressed but dutiful: they would be "willing to observe mainstream norms like work if only government will enforce them". Yet in Mead's scheme of things, non-working adults want to work but do not work consistently. Some resist taking available jobs because they deem them to be unfair. Others feel overwhelmed by the practical difficulties presented by employment.

In many respects, this interpretation by Mead tended to temper the excesses of Murray's deliberations. In one sense, Mead's notion of the poor resisting available jobs agrees with Murray's rational, calculative hypothesis. In another sense, Mead was showing an (albeit limited) understanding of the probable difficulties and subsequent inadequacies encountered and experienced by the poor. Effectively, Mead was producing a more comprehensive (in terms of understanding) interpretation of the 'underclass' than the interpretation put forward by Murray. Nevertheless, this is not to suggest that Mead did not agree with Murray's view of the 'underclass' as a growing social problem; nor is it an assertion that he disagreed with Murray in the belief that unconditional welfare was exacerbating the situation. On the contrary, this disagreement over the essence of human nature only manifested itself in the respective prescriptions each advocated as a cure. For Mead, the solution did not lie in Murray's ruthless quest to repeal all welfare payments to the members of this 'underclass'. Rather, Mead (1986, p 81) argued that:

> What is missing is the idea of obligation. Work is normative for the poor, but it is not something they feel they *must* do, whatever the personal cost.

Arguably, the inclusion of obligation in welfare policy provided government officials on both sides of the Atlantic with a more pragmatic weapon to tackle the perceived problem of the 'underclass'. Obligation, therefore, provides this book with Mead's second aspect of importance. Through the attachment of obligation to welfare policies, the draconian harshness of Murray's withdrawal of welfare for all but the infirm and disabled is tempered and made less unpalatable to many. At least with the inclusion of obligation into welfare schemes a government can be seen to be helping individuals rather than simply leaving them to fend for themselves. Conditionality in this respect represents an attempt to reform the poor and is not simply punitive. For Mead, and of course the supporters of the welfare-to-work schemes discussed later in this book, the link between social rights and compulsory responsibilities is a positive step in that it attempts to bring "the poor back into the citizenship fold" (Dwyer, 2000a, p 66). From this perspective, such schemes could not be accused of providing 'perverse incentives'. Neither could they be seen to be inhumane on the one hand or ineffective on the other.

The third and final aspect of importance this book attaches to Mead lay in his use of language and his terminology. Throughout his discussions of the poor, Mead directly relates dependency to dysfunctionality. In this sense, Mead's interpretation contrasts with that of Murray. Nonetheless the two positions are compatible. Similarly, each is supportive of the basic premises that lay behind functionalist theory in general. Specifically, Murray does not see the 'underclass' as being dysfunctional per se; after all, they make rational choices and act accordingly. However, his description of the 'underclass' reinforces the functionalist image of how an industrious and prosperous society is envisaged to operate. To reiterate, Murray's depiction of a member of the 'underclass' is the antithesis of the good 'citizens' of this world who work hard, are fundamentally honest and come from a 'stable' family background. Good citizens are functional within the system of capitalism and not dysfunctional to it.

Mead opened the door to functionalism even further. As stated earlier, Mead disputes that all the poor are capable of making rational choices. Some individuals, but not all, simply cannot cope with employment. Consequently, the chief question facing social policy is "how far government should control the lives of dysfunctional people in their own interests" (Mead, 1991, p 9). Clearly, Mead's recognition that certain individuals cannot cope – and his subsequent image of individuals being dysfunctional – brings the 'underclass' debate firmly within the realms of functionalist theory. Again, we have the preconceived idea of what is functional. Again, the implication is that hard work and morality enable individuals to contribute to a successful and harmonious society.

Responsibilities, communitarian compatibility and initial policy manifestations

Nonetheless, the connection between the 'underclass' debate and the thoughts and ideas associated with functionalism does not end with Mead's reference to dysfunctionality alone. On the contrary, the views and prescriptions of Murray and Mead show a remarkable similarity to those of the new communitarian movement. In an attempt to summarise the debate west of the Atlantic, for instance, David T. Ellwood provided an invaluable insight into how the two strands of thought can be associated with each other. In his summary, Ellwood identified "four basic tenets that seem[ed] to underlie much of the American philosophical and political rhetoric about poverty [and which] in turn present[ed] three difficult dilemmas for welfare policy makers" (Walker, 1991, p 9). In essence, the four basic tenets were:

- a fundamental belief in the *autonomy of the individual*;
- a promotion of the work ethic with the promulgation of the *virtue of work*;
- the elevation of the *primacy of the family*;

- last, but not least, a *desire for and sense of community* (Ellwood, 1988, p 16).

In contrast, the three dilemmas faced by such social policy revolved around the conundrums arising out of the reduced incentives/pressures on the poor to work and care for themselves when people are given money, food or housing (Ellwood, 1988, p 19); out of the changes induced in the family structure when assistance is oriented towards the more vulnerable single-parent families (1988, pp 20-1); and lastly, out of the isolation that the 'truly needy' have to endure from labelling and stigmatisation that accompanies any targeting of the poorest sections of the community (1988, pp 23-5).

The compatibility with the communitarian agenda discussed in Chapter Three is plain to see. As we have seen in Chapter Three, communitarians argue that the revival of institutions such as the 'family', 'school', 'workplace', 'neighbourhood' and 'community' would rediscover an ethical basis for politics and so provide individuals with a sense of mutual responsibility. In this light, the notion of communities that "chastise those who violate shared moral norms and express approbation for those who abide by them" (Etzioni, 1995, p ix) points to a fundamental belief that a common sense of 'duty' and 'obligation' has to be reinforced, if not restored, to the modern way of living. Likewise, this reflects the previously discussed concern over individual demands for 'rights' at the expense of 'responsibilities'. Clearly, this stance is compatible with that of Murray who argues that the UK and the US are being overrun by a growing 'underclass' that is characteristically irresponsible, immoral and, in the supplementary words of Mead, dysfunctional. Paid work, and the belief that this would actively promote feelings of responsibility and a real sense of community, thus provides a focal point of similarity where the works of Murray, Mead and Etzioni can be attuned to each other.

Indeed, it was within the climate of these debates – and in the shadow of a long history of disparate, regional welfare-to-work measures in the US – that the Reagan administration first attempted a series of legislation designed to enforce the principles of 'workfare' nationwide. In 1981, the Republicans unsuccessfully proposed to replace the more or less voluntary Work Incentive Scheme – which used "financial incentives, training and counselling to stimulate labour market participation" (Ellwood, 1988, p 16) – with a compulsory Community Work Experience Program. They failed because Congress refused to mandate states to introduce 'workfare'.

Nevertheless, between 1981 and 1984, Congress did, in fact, authorise a set of four welfare-to-work alternatives that operated until 1988. One such option was the Compulsory Work Experience Program itself. This was 'true workfare' under which the recipients of the means-tested Aid to Families with Dependent Children (AFDC) were required to perform purposeful, unpaid work in exchange for welfare benefit, but not at the expense of regular work or workers (Ellwood, 1988, p 17). Another choice was the Title IV – A Job Search option. In this case, those receiving AFDC benefit were required to participate in an individual or collective job search for a minimum period of 16 weeks in their first year, and for eight weeks each year thereafter. The third alternative was Work Supplementation, where the recipient's AFDC grant subsidised the payment of a standard wage in return for on-the-job training given by a private, or public employer. Finally, the fourth was a single-agency Work Incentive Scheme (WIN) in which "a more flexible variant of WIN operated at a local level by the welfare agency (and at Federal level by the Family Support Administration in the DHHS [Department of Health and Human Services])" (Ellwood, 1988, p 17).

As a consequence of this available range of policy choice, and the noticeable complication of the continuation of the WIN scheme alongside a "central commitment to flexibility at state level", there was not only a diversity of piecemeal, often contradictory schemes from state to state, but, more disturbingly for Reagan and his followers, there appeared to be a distinct "lack of overall program direction" (US General Accounting Office, 1987, quoted in Walker, 1991, p 17). Accordingly, in an unashamedly draconian response, the Family Support Act was signed into law by President Reagan on 13 October 1988. Title II of this act, the Jobs Opportunities and Basic Skills Training Program (JOBS), "established in federal law a mandatory reform such that each of the fifty states [were] required to apply welfare-work programs to welfare recipients" (King, 1995, p 173).

A comprehensive and – as may be noticed in the UK and New Labour's most recent policy documents – a highly influential precedent had been set. To wit each state, after October 1990, was compelled to design, and implement a fivefold JOBS programme of services. These services were to consist of:

- educational activities to provide English as a second language and a literacy level equivalent to high-school graduation;
- job skills training;
- job readiness programmes;
- job development and placement facilities;

- and, in keeping with the diagnosis of an 'underclass' containing single mothers and their illegitimate offspring, childcare and transportation support mechanisms.

For the work requirement component, states were bound to offer two out of four possible options. The first was job-search assistance; the second embodied on-the-job training; whereas the third encompassed the previously described system of subsidised labour in Work Supplementation. In a like manner, the fourth alternative presented the Community Work Experience Program as a formal option for all the states of the union (King, 1995, p 174). From this point on, the correlation between welfare, work and the problem of dealing with the 'feckless' unemployed, was firmly entrenched within the social policy agenda of America.

Similar debates and experiences in Britain eventually contributed to the evolution of New Labour policy. The first public manifestation of which occurred in 1988, when John Moore, then Secretary of State for Social Security in the Conservative administration, warned the Conservative Party Conference that "we have to continue to work on the connection between benefits and behaviour.... We have to continue the fight to solve the age old problem: how to help someone without weakening his will to help himself" (Moore, 1988, p 12). It was an open declaration that the views of Murray, Mead and Ellwood were to be taken seriously in Britain. Effectively, John Moore had provided one of the first indications that such views would, by 1989 at least, begin to permeate the political consciousness of Britain through the actions and deliberations of the Conservative Party.

Notwithstanding the overwhelming Conservative drive to cut social security costs, practical demonstrations of this new-found direction took three distinct forms. One aspect related to the perceived problems associated with the 'perverse incentives' of welfare support. Moves to rectify the problems of the 'poverty trap' could be seen in Conservative attempts at rationalising the relationship between Housing Benefit, Supplementary Benefit and Family Income Supplement. With the Social Security Act of 1986, Housing Benefit was sharply cut back and only paid to those close to the levels of the new Income Support that had replaced Supplementary Benefit. In turn, Family Credit was introduced to replace the Family Income Supplement for those in work. Throughout, the same criteria for means testing were to be applied. In the case of Family Credit, the test would only be applied to post-tax income. Ultimately, it became virtually impossible for anyone to lose more than 100% of each extra pound earned as a consequence of the withdrawal of benefits and increased taxation. As a result, "[t]he poverty trap ... had been made wider, but shallower" (Timmins, 1996, p 401).

Importantly, however, the inclusion of a work qualification for Family Credit (of 24 hours or less) demonstrated a desire to promote work and family values. Low-paid families could now avoid the 'poverty trap' by remaining (or becoming) participants in the economy. The second aspect of this Conservative change of direction entailed a further reinforcement of these 'missing' family values. The original Conservative proposals for the creation of the Child Support Agency, with its uncompromising powers, was intended to be the vehicle for Murray inspired Thatcherite ideals where "no father should be able to escape from his responsibility" (Margaret Thatcher quoted in Timmins, 1996, p 452). In its rudimentary form, it was specifically designed to counter the dramatic increase in the number of lone parents in Britain. Priority was to be given to the first partner, and offspring, in a direct attack upon separation, divorce and, more intensely, upon illegitimacy.

The other example emerged in September 1988 when the right to income support for all 16 and 17 year olds, not in work or education, was withdrawn as a guaranteed package to provide Youth Training Scheme (YTS) places. It produced a 6% cut in means-tested benefits and, arguably, represented the first step towards the removal of 'unconditional' rights to benefit. The later implementation of adult training schemes, and the more recent Job Seeker's Allowance, which "cuts the rights to benefits after 6 months instead of 12" (Milne, 1997, p 13) elaborated upon this theme. As Chapter Six of this volume will substantiate, the scene was thus set for New Labour to implement further authoritarian measures similar to those advocated by the social 'moralists' of the US.

Murray and functionalist ideas

At the beginning of this chapter, it was pointed out that ideas could only become policy if they had the ability to appeal to a number of different constituencies or areas of interest (Mann and Roseneil, 1994). A re-evaluation of the evidence recorded so far would demonstrate this to be particularly true of the ideas and thoughts of Charles Murray. In part, it has to be acknowledged that the ideas of Murray survived simply because some mothers were deliberately having illegitimate children in order to claim welfare benefits (Field, 1993; Phillips, 1993; Mann and Roseneil, 1994). This, as the book has demonstrated, was abhorrent to many (particularly in the New Right) and had to be countered; hence the initial articulations of concern and empathy for Murray's views. Nevertheless, it has become clear that Murray's deliberations extend beyond mere articulation, concern and empathy. In truth, the approach of Murray has become firmly manifest in actual social policies implemented on both sides of the Atlantic. Primarily, this has occurred as a direct consequence of the instrumental value such ideas have given to a variety of different protagonists and discourses. In effect, Murray's analysis of the 'underclass' provided a significant platform upon which a variety of patriarchal, fiscal and ideological attacks on the 'underclass' could be launched (see Mann and Roseneil, 1994).

On the whole, lone mothers were being seen as the root cause of the problem itself. Besides being victims of an increase in the feminisation of poverty (see Rodgers, 1986; Graham, 1993; Dey, 1996), lone mothers were also falling prey to what Hall et al (1978) identified elsewhere as a 'moral panic'. In effect, there was a growing sense of alarm over never-married mothers as the root cause of increased juvenile crime, intergenerational welfare dependency and the complete rejection of the norms and values of mainstream society (see Bagguley and Mann, 1992; Murray, 1996a, 1996b). To reiterate once more, the words of Murray have appealed to numerous quarters in both British and American society. Importantly for this book, Murray's appeal also extends to those who take a functionalist view of capitalism. When allied to communitarianism and Mead's more moderate but equally draconian prescription of 'obligation' as a proviso for the receipt of welfare, Murray's basic premise provided an essential foundation stone for the welfare-to-work policies introduced in Britain since 1997. In this respect, Chapter Six – through direct reference to the New Deals set in place by New Labour – will demonstrate how so-called 'dysfunctional' individuals could possibly be brought back into line. By doing so, it will further cement the compatibility of Murray's discourse to the overarching functionalist discourse of New Labour.

SIX

Functionalism and the 'third way': work, 'opportunity' and New Labour's support for the 'family' institution

Introduction

So far, this book has charted the development and progression of structural-functionalism from the early musings of Talcott Parsons to the communitarianism of Amitai Etzioni. It has also taken note of the complementary and, indeed, compatible discourses such as those surrounding the 'underclass' debate characterised by Charles Murray, Lawrence Mead and David Ellwood. Mixed in with all of this has been a discussion of the work of John Macmurray who, in the view of Hale (2002), can be described as Tony Blair's self-declared guru that never was. And with this work it has been possible to glean the dominant influence of communitarianism – as opposed to Macmurray's egalitarian musings – on the policies and thoughts of Tony Blair and New Labour. With the exception of Macmurray (and perhaps Charles Murray's more distressing analysis), it has become apparent throughout that most of these differing viewpoints share a common view of capitalism. In particular, they see capitalism as a motivational benign hierarchy that is best suited to promote prosperous and harmonious human relations. In sum, we have begun to unravel the entangled web of complementary ideas that underpin the functionalism behind the policies of New Labour.

In this chapter, the process of discovery takes a step further. Initially, the chapter discusses the 'third way' and how it represents a clear manifestation of communitarian beliefs. By implication, this also represents another demonstration of New Labour's functionalism. Later, it addresses New Labour's penchant to give primacy to the concept of 'equality of opportunity'. As will become apparent, this is also premised upon visions of a benevolent arena of competition in an equally benign social hierarchy. Again, this reflects an underlying reliance upon functionalist trains of thought. Finally, this chapter will begin to reveal the actual policy realisations arising out of these deliberations. Most prominently, it will introduce the reasoning behind the work oriented New Deal schemes and cement them within the context of 'Blair's communitarianisms'. In so doing, the ground is thus laid open for Chapter Seven's concluding discussion of the possible pitfalls that may beset such schemes.

Anthony Giddens and the 'third way' to a better society

Any discussion of New Labour would not be complete without a mention of Anthony Giddens. Giddens is of particular importance to this book on two fronts. On the first, Giddens' now relinquished position as Director of the London School of Economics (LSE) had enabled him to exert a significant influence on the thoughts of Tony Blair (see Mann, 2001; Prideaux, 2001; Cammack, 2004; Morrison, 2004). On the second and directly related front, Giddens (1994, 1998, 2000) has written extensively on what is now famously called the 'third way'. On this score, both he and Blair:

> believe that the essence of the third way lies in the need to adapt the traditional values of the centre left to contemporary social and economic conditions. (Deacon, 2002, p 103)

As Giddens succinctly put it in *The Observer* (1998b, in Lavalette and Mooney, 2000, p 35):

> The overall aim of Third Way politics should be to help citizens plot their way through the major revolutions of our time: globalisation, transformations in personal life and our relationship to nature. Third Way politics should preserve a core concern with social justice, while accepting that the range of questions which escape the left/right divide is greater than before. Freedom to social democrats should mean autonomy of action, which in turn demands the involvement of the wider social community. Having abandoned collectivism, Third Way politics looks for a new relationship between the individual and community, a redefinition of rights and obligations.

With specific regard to the delivery of welfare, such conceptualisations of the 'third way' primarily require the state to fulfil a threefold purpose. First, argues Giddens, the state is obliged to create a society in which work (specifically meaning paid labour in industry) has a central defining role. Second, the state must foster 'national solidarity', whereas the third directs the state towards the management of risk (Giddens, 1994). According to Wetherly (2001), the first obviously relates to the efficiency aspect of welfare in that it entails the reinforcement of work incentives and labour market participation. The second, he continues (2001, p 152), addresses notions of social justice "in the sense that citizenship in the form of common social, as well as civil and political, rights promotes social cohesion". Linked to this is the third purpose that expresses elements of social justice in so far as the risks facing all citizens have to be confronted. As a consequence, 'risk management' is acutely pertinent to the provision of welfare services, especially to those services that cater for the basic needs surrounding health, welfare and education.

Taken in this context, such objectives can only be met through a fundamental shift in the way in which welfare is conceived, delivered and subsequently received. Initially, the state must jettison the top-down redistribution approach of previous years and replace it with a system of 'social investment'. Only with 'social investment', it is stressed, would the state be capable of meeting its responsibility to ensure social justice through the provision of 'opportunity' rather than through a redistribution of wealth (Giddens, 1994, 1998; Dwyer, 2000a). On the flip side of the same coin, these state responsibilities have to be matched with individual responsibilities. As Giddens himself put it (2003, p 37), one "might suggest as a prime motto for the new politics, *no rights without responsibilities*".

Alongside today's expanding individualism, continues Giddens, must come an extension of individual obligations. No longer is it possible or desirable for rights to be treated as unconditional claims. Unemployment benefits, for example, should be tied with an obligation to actively look for work. Governments should not discourage active search, they should promote it through "positive welfare oriented to manufactured rather than external risk" (Giddens, 1994, p 192). In this respect, government provision would primarily be aimed at:

> fostering the *autotelic self* [who would be] a person able to translate potential threats into rewarding challenges, someone ... able to turn entropy into a consistent flow of

> experience ... as [part of] the active challenge which
> generates *self-actualisation*. (1994, p 192)

Ultimately, the 'self-actualised individual' would achieve self-fulfilment as they transcend egotism and selfishness and so be at peace with him or herself (see Hayes, 1998). In sum, these individuals would have no obsessive desire to dominate others or to exercise power over them. Instead, they would rise above personal avarice and exploitative behaviour as they pursue individual aims that are set alongside social obligations.

However, in order to promote the 'self-actualisation' process even further, Giddens contends that these 'positive' forms of social investment should also be applied throughout the whole of the social security network. Taken in conjunction with the changes in unemployment benefit, such an extension of application would significantly help to alleviate increasing expenditure problems faced by government. In particular, Giddens pays specific attention to the contemporary problems posed by an increasingly older population and the growing financial demand for pensions. For Giddens, the essence of the problem stems from the way in which old age was conceptualised during the formation of the welfare state. The notion of a pension that begins at the retirement age of 60 or 65, and the label of 'pensioner', are, in the eyes of Giddens, clear inventions of the welfare state. Pensioners were perceived by the welfare state "as clear a case of welfare dependency as one can find" (Giddens, 1998, p 120). Yet these conceptions do not conform to the realities of modern life. People now live longer and, unlike in the past, ageing no longer represents an inert occurrence. Nor is the ageing body simply accepted. In the more active, reflexive society of today, ageing has, for Giddens (1998, p 119) at least, "become much more of an open process, on a physical as well as a psychic level". Indeed:

> Ageing is a much more diverse and actively shaped process
> than it used to be – in common with other areas of life in
> a globalising era, what it is to be an 'older person' is more
> ... negotiable. Even the body doesn't passively 'age' any
> longer, but can be influenced by habits, diet and a person's
> approach to life. (2000, pp 39-40)

Consequently, original conceptualisations of old age are no longer relevant. Therefore, the way in which retirement and the age of retirement are envisaged by both the state and the individual has to be reconstituted if a solution to the problems is to be found.

According to Giddens, the first step towards a solution can be taken with the abolition of the fixed age of retirement. By doing so, individuals would be free from the artificial confines of being a 'pensioner' and its associations with welfare dependency, incapacity and, in many cases, the loss of self-esteem. Effectively, we should "regard older people as a resource rather than a problem" (Giddens, 1998, p 120). As a result, the category of a 'pensioner' would cease to exist because pensions would then become detachable from the notion of a 'pensionable age'. Instead, people should be allowed to use their pension fund as they so wish since it makes no sense to lock up such funds until the traditional age of retirement has been reached. In this way, it would be possible for individuals of the future either to leave the labour force at any age of their choosing, finance their own education/further education or reduce their working hours when bringing up children.

These new arrangements, however, would not have a negative effect upon the economy. From Giddens' perspective, they would probably have a more neutral impact upon the labour market. Yes, it is a possibility that individuals could give up work earlier, but conversely it is also possible that other individuals could and should be encouraged to stay in work much longer. In this latter respect, Giddens (1998, p 120) emphasises the point that any "society that separates older people from the majority in a retirement ghetto cannot be inclusive". Thus society has a duty to actively include the older generation. As always, though, the duties of society and the state have to be matched by the duties expected of the individual. In Giddens' words (1998, p 121), the "precept of philosophic conservatism applies here as elsewhere: old age shouldn't be seen as a time of rights without responsibilities". Rather, it should be the responsibility of the older generation to set an example to the younger elements of society. Through an 'intergenerational contract', adds Giddens, the older generation should see themselves as being in the service of future generations and act accordingly.

In return, this contract between the generations would also oblige the young to look to the old for a model on how to conduct their lives. For Giddens, such a contract would be a realistic and workable proposition simply because of the already stated fact that being old now lasts longer. With this contemporary extension of old age, concludes Giddens, there is the inevitable reality of far more old people in the population. As a consequence, "the old are more socially visible" (1998, p 121) and their previously suggested increase in involvement in work and the community would thus act to link them directly to younger generations. Hence the perceived feasibility of Giddens' 'intergenerational contract'; hence Giddens' push to counter the demand for 'rights' with a similar drive to restore the notion of collective and personal 'responsibility'.

A five-point blueprint to 'democratise democracy'

Notwithstanding the positive advantages perceived to arise out of the changes in how welfare should be delivered and received (whether it be in the form of social security benefits or state pensions), Giddens also maintains that individual responsibility cannot remain confined to the recipients of welfare alone. Indeed, the opposite has to be the case: the association of rights with responsibilities must apply to everyone and not apply only to the old, "the poor or the needy" (Giddens, 2003, p 37). In this respect, a more universal application of responsibility can only be reinforced and promoted if a new framework of reference has also been established for the state and civil society to operate within. Consequently for Giddens (1998, p 70), the notion of positive welfare – and what amounts to a "social investment state" – can only flourish under the auspices of an innovative 'radical centre' in the political arena and, importantly, through the concomitant development of a "new democratic state (the state without enemies)" that encourages 'self-actualisation' and a subsequent promotion of an active civil society. Likewise, for the active civil society to prosper, it is also necessary to promote the ideal of a "democratic family" whose working patterns and shared responsibilities enable it to both thrive upon, and contribute to, what Giddens envisages as a "new mixed economy" based upon the principle of "equality as inclusion" (1998, p 70).

In an attempt to move away from the subjectivity of such a framework, Giddens (2003, p 37) takes great care to explain that a 'new democratic state', for instance, could only arise out of the modern precept of "*no authority without democracy*". With a concerted five-point blueprint to "democratise democracy" (1998, p 72), Giddens argues that it is first necessary for the state to respond structurally to globalisation. Implicitly for Giddens, the process of 'democratising democracy' involves decentralisation. Nevertheless, this decentralisation should not be a one-way process. More, the state's response to globalisation should constitute "a movement of double democratisation" (Giddens, 1998, p 72) whereby power is not only devolved to the regions and localities, but also where democratic power is simultaneously transferred "upwards, above the level of the nation state" (Giddens, 2000, p 62). In due course, the authority of the nation-state would be strengthened rather than weakened by this double movement in the democratic procedure. As a result, concludes Giddens (1998, p 72), authority would be reasserted as the state becomes more responsive "to the influences that otherwise outflank it all round".

With the second aspect of his blueprint, Giddens concerns himself with the public sphere. To be specific, he advocates that the state should expand the role of the public sphere through constitutional reform aimed not only at providing new safeguards against corruption, but also to promote a greater transparency and openness of dealings and operations. For Giddens, the need for this constitutional reform arises because governments throughout the world are the recipients of more detailed attention. It is simply not the case that corruption within government is generally on the increase. On the contrary, one of the most significant changes affecting the political sphere is that the single information environment that we all now live in brings the existing ways of doing things under closer scrutiny. As a direct result, "the scope of what is seen as corrupt or unacceptable widens" (Giddens, 1998, p 73).

In Britain, the need for constitutional reform is seen to be particularly acute. Unlike all other liberal democracies, reflects Giddens, Britain does not have a written constitution. Only in custom and to an extent in case law are the functions of government set alongside the rights and duties of citizens. In this light, constitutional change must not only aim to make the principles of democracy more explicit, but also reform has to counter the culture of secrecy that is pervading the higher levels of British institutions. It is essential that reform is able to lessen the power of the executive. At the same time, existing forms of accountability have to be greatly strengthened if democracy is to succeed in the modern world. No longer is it acceptable for parliamentary committees to merely "reflect the composition of the Commons" (Giddens, 1998, p 74). Nor, adds Giddens (2000, p 62), is it permissible for old-boy networks, "backstage deals, unashamed forms of patronage", and the anachronism of the House of Lords to continue. In short, the entrenched ways of doing things have to be actively and directly confronted.

Third in Giddens' blueprint to 'democratise democracy' is the need for "states without enemies" (1998, p 74) to elevate their administrative efficiency. Only by doing this can a state retain or regain its legitimacy in the face of the increased mistrust the modern political culture has for large bureaucracies. Moreover, suggests Giddens, many of today's citizens see local and regional government as able to meet their needs more effectively than the national state. Hierarchy and the traditional symbols and trappings of power are viewed with suspicion and, as a consequence, there is greater support for an increase in the role of "non-profit voluntary agencies in the delivery of public services" (2000, p 42) as opposed to more traditional forms of governmental provision.

Although Giddens does not see the trend towards decentralisation and the recruitment of non-government organisations as necessarily a negative thing, he does, nonetheless, hold the view that most governments still have "a good deal to learn from business best practice" (1998, p 74). Target controls, effective auditing, flexible decision structures and increased employee participation can all play a significant part in a government-led response to the criticism that state institutions have become lazy, lack market discipline and deliver shoddy services. However, in a caveat typical of the 'third way', Giddens moves on to stress that an appropriate response is not simply to introduce market mechanisms or quasi-markets wherever and whenever the opportunity presents itself. Quite the opposite: the process of reinventing government may well mean adopting market-based solutions when the need arises, but "it also should mean reasserting the effectiveness of government in the face of markets" (Giddens, 1998, p 75).

The fourth point Giddens has to make relates to the possibility of implementing other forms of democracy apart from the orthodox process of voting. The downward pressure engendered by globalisation, he notes, provides the opportunity for governments to experiment with democracy. The possible introduction of local direct democracy, electronic referenda and citizens' juries, continues Giddens, can serve to complement – rather than substitute for – normal voting mechanisms and, in doing so, be of immense importance in a government's quest to re-establish a more direct contact with its citizens.

Naturally, such moves will help to maintain if not secure legitimacy for a government. For Giddens, however, 'states without enemies' can also reinforce their legitimacy through their capacity to manage risk. Management of risk for the 'third way', of course, is not solely restricted to the welfare state's traditional provision of social security alone. Neither does it simply concern economic matters. Other risks, namely those coming from science and technology also impinge directly upon government. Global warming or the possible dangers presented by genetically modified foods, for instance, present governments with serious problems over legitimacy if they are unable or unwilling to manage and regulate developments. Sooner than the state acting as the 'insurer of last resort', remarks Giddens (2000, p 139), government should "seek to democratise science and technology, as part of the project of 'democratising democracy'". Risk simply cannot be left solely to experts. Science and technology "can no longer be left outside the scope of democracy, since they influence our lives in a more direct and far-reaching way than was true for previous generations" (Giddens, 2003, p 38). From the beginning, then, public involvement – through the establishment of deliberative procedures involving government, experts and lay individuals – is required so that trust can be (re-) established as the practical choices and the limits of available scientific or technical knowledge are illuminated.

Crucially, this coalition of governments, experts and lay-people exemplifies the logic and circularity of Giddens' deliberations. To complement and reinforce the overall process of 'double democracy', for example, Giddens returns to the desire for third-way politics to foster an 'active civil society'. Not only can the newly democratised 'investment state' encourage and instil personal and collective responsibility but, as the discussion of science and technology seems to suggest, a government intent on taking the 'third way' can also promote the idea that it is possible for individuals to act in partnership with the state in all areas of modern life. Even so, such individuals should not have to act in isolation from others. On the contrary, the politics of the 'third way' can only be successfully applied if a sense of 'community' throughout civil society is effectively revived. And to achieve this, practical means have to be found to further "the social and material refurbishment of neighbourhoods, towns and larger local areas" (Giddens, 1998, p 78).

Taking the communitarian path beyond Left and Right

When it comes to considering the actual practicalities of refurbishing poorer neighbourhoods, however, Giddens stipulates that this should not refer to government provision alone. As before, Giddens stresses that the state and civil society should act in partnership to facilitate and regulate each other. There should be, he emphasises, no permanent boundaries between government and civil society. Occasionally, a government needs to be involved deeply in the civil arena. Sometimes, a government also needs to retreat. Context and flexibility are all important. Indeed, where a government refrains or retracts from direct involvement, its resources might still be necessary to support activities that local groups may introduce or take over. Overall, however, Giddens believes that any diminution in reliance or trust shown to politicians and other authority figures is not an issue of undue concern. It is not, he speculates, an indication of social apathy. Quite the reverse:

> [a] reflexive society is also one marked by high-levels of self-organisation. (Giddens, 1998, p 80)

For Giddens, self-organisation represents a crucial aspect in the quest to revive 'community'. In America and in the UK, he observes, research indicates that there is a burgeoning civil sphere whereby older, more traditional forms of civil association and civic engagement are being replaced by other forms of communal energy. In this light, it is both logical and essential that such alternative energies are harnessed "to wider social ends in ways that benefit local communities as well as society as a whole" (1998, p 80). Giddens reasons that one way of harnessing these energies would be to encourage the greater involvement of the voluntary sector and charitable groups in public affairs. Encouragement of local initiatives (fortified by external support and resources) and 'social entrepreneurship', therefore, represent the first step to solving the problems of marginalisation and economic decline.

Giddens is convinced that poorer areas in Britain would benefit enormously from the adoption of similar schemes already in place in Brazil, the US and Japan. In Brazil, the reforms enacted on behalf of the indigenous population of Ceara represent a prime example. Young reformers from business, television and retail in this area joined with government agencies, utilised a variety of participatory planning techniques and cooperated with community organisations in a concerted attempt to raise wage levels and overcome the greed of the traditional elites. New schemes were introduced specifically to encourage fresh enterprise. Families with the greatest need were allocated one minimum-wage job per household. Day care centres were set up and run by volunteers guaranteed at least the minimum wage, while neighbourhood groups were given resources to lend on a small scale. As a result, Ceara's economy, between 1987 and 1994, grew "at a rate of 4 per cent, compared with 1.4 per cent for Brazil as a whole" (Giddens, 1998, p 83).

Pointing to developments elsewhere, Giddens expands upon the Brazilian example to argue that 'social entrepreneurship' represents another important aspect in the pursuit to revitalise a community atmosphere. To be specific, Giddens champions the virtues of the concept of 'service credit', which he claims has been introduced to a range of cities in the US and Japan. With 'service credit', he ventures, collective responsibility and, to a lesser extent, the principle of 'self-help' is nurtured by volunteers who donate their time and energies in return for reciprocal payments of time donated by other volunteer workers. In turn, each donation of time represents a deposit or expenditure of a 'time dollar' from the registered 'personal' accounts related to the respective participants involved. Crucially for the success of this scheme, 'time dollars' are tax-free and can be accumulated to an extent that they may be used to pay for "health care as well as other health services, including reducing health insurance costs" (1998, p 83).

In a similar fashion, these 'time dollars' can also be used to help pay for educational needs or serve as a resource during a period of unemployment. In the long run, these 'time dollar' programmes would effectively create a "volunteered time economy" (1998, p 84) that would redress the perceived imbalance between rights and responsibilities. Set out in these terms, social or rather civic entrepreneurs would form the basis of Giddens'new mixed economy' in which the zeal and creativity of traditional entrepreneurs in the laissez-faire market is brought into the public sector. Instead of prohibiting these voluntary endeavours, the role of government should thus be to encourage and contribute to such activities. As Giddens (2000, pp 6-7) explicitly stipulates, "the state should not row, but steer: not so much control as challenge.... A positive climate for entrepreneurial independence and initiative has to be nurtured".

Conversely, this 'new mixed economy' cannot prosper from government encouragement alone. For Giddens, it is imperative that the family – his "basic institution of civil society" (1998, p 89) and responsible behaviour – is reinvigorated in a way that will go beyond the political interpretations of the New Right and old-style social democracy. By starting from the premise that children "who grow up in a household with only one biological parent are worse off, on average, than children who grow up in a household with both of their biological parents" (2000, p 47), Giddens proceeds to argue that government should foster conditions in which individuals would be able to form stable ties with others. The 'democratised family', he concludes, signifies the way forward.

As with 'double democracy' in the public sphere, the reconstituted democratic family shares similar characteristics. To be specific, this implies the need for families to establish emotional and sexual equality, mutual rights and responsibilities in relationships and, importantly for Giddens, an increased emphasis on co-parenting. Indeed, co-parenting for Giddens entails lifelong parental contracts, negotiated authority over children and the obligations of children to parents. All would reflect a concerted attempt to establish a "socially integrated family" (Giddens, 1998, p 95) that is capable of participating in – and responsibly contributing to – the continued development of a truly democratic society premised on the politics of the 'third way'.

In spite of the lack of substantive detail behind his overarching propositions, the most striking aspect of Giddens' theoretical constructions is the ability to manipulate hitherto conflicting stances and theories. Rights, for instance, are prominently placed alongside responsibilities. Socialism is set against neo-liberalism while egalitarianism is positioned alongside individualism (Giddens, 1998, 2000, 2003). Likewise, the public sector is measured by the achievements of the corporate and voluntary sectors in order to strengthen calls for 'partnership'. Yet, implicit within all of this is the belief that it is not a government's role to simply provide for its citizens in the established way of the traditional welfare state. As opposed to advocating the redistribution of wealth or equality of outcome, the emphasis shifts towards the provision of 'opportunity' to all citizens. Certainly, this 'equality of opportunity', as Giddens (2000) describes it later, becomes a centrepiece for 'third way' politics. Typically, Giddens (2000, p 86) stresses that the Left have to learn to approve:

> its correlates – that incentives are necessary to encourage those of talent to progress and that equality of opportunity … creates higher rather than lower inequalities of outcome. Equality of opportunity also tends to produce high levels of social and cultural diversity, since individuals and groups have a chance to develop their lives as they see fit.… Rather than seeking to suppress these consequences we should accept them.

By now, the language, tone and meaning of the statements and deliberations of Giddens should seem remarkably familiar. As with organisational theory and structural-functionalism before it, a benign view of capitalism (now placed under a global umbrella) is positively accepted. Inequality is deemed to be positive, whereas the relationship between the individual, family and community initially raised by Etzioni in Chapter Three is again brought to the fore. Similarly, Giddens' talk of balancing rights with responsibilities is perfectly in tune with the characteristic message of the two communitarian bibles: *The spirit of community* (1995) and *The new golden rule* (1997). Equally, the declared desire of Giddens to resuscitate a sense of community through the prescription of an intergenerational contract, increased participation in the paid labour market and the advocacy for voluntary action in the more deprived areas of society could easily have come from the mouth of Etzioni himself.

New Labour and the primacy of 'opportunity'

At first glance, the earlier discussion of the theoretical position of Giddens suggests that a connection with structural-functionalism can be established through the association Etzioni's communitarianism has with organisational theory. Yet, before this aspect can be fully addressed in the last section of this chapter, it is important to note that the emphasis Giddens places upon the provision of 'opportunities' also provides a link with the thoughts of Parsons, Merton and Davis and Moore. When viewed in this light, Giddens thus provides the initial opening for the book to discuss how New Labour has also adopted a like-minded approach. Certainly the aforementioned influence that Giddens had as director of the LSE directly suggests that his deliberations have, in actual fact, become a part of New Labour's theoretical standpoint. Indeed, the underlying assumptions of the 'New Deal' schemes also suggest that this is so.

Before the General Election of 1997, for instance, New Labour's self-styled brand of 'socialism' was, much in the mould of Giddens, conspicuously defined as 'equality of opportunity'. Indeed, Raymond Plant (1993, pp 11-12), a leading thinker of the 'Left' and front bench Labour peer, stipulated that:

> it would be irrational to prefer a more equal distribution of resources which left everyone, including the poor, worse off than they could be under a system in which there would be some inequalities but which would also benefit the poor ... we can get a fairer distribution of resources and opportunities.

This implicit acceptance of 'inequality' – regardless of any moral belief in the notion that wealth would 'trickle down' – reflected New Labour's willingness to embrace the concept of society as a competitive hierarchy motivated by 'aspiration'. In turn, this 'aspirational' politics acted to suppress the more 'radical' policies and principles of the Labour movement past and present.

On the basis of this train of thought, it became entirely consistent for 'Shadow Chancellor' Gordon Brown (1994, p 3) to envisage that his 'mission' was to build "a fair society in which all people, regardless of class, race or gender have available to them the widest choice of options and opportunities to enhance their earning power and fulfil their true potential". Plant's redistribution of 'resources and opportunities' had now become purely the allocation of those resources in order to provide 'opportunity'. Resources as such would no longer be directly spent on the individual in the form of unconditional benefits. Rather, available resources would be used to provide individuals with an opening back into the labour market.

With this form of logic, Gordon Brown was released from the 'redistributionist' policies of old to postulate that the welfare state should and could be reorganised to provide 'pathways' out of unemployment, poverty and, ultimately, crime (Brown, 1994, pp 4-5). As a result, the disadvantaged and the unemployed would be able to meet their 'aspirational needs' as they pass through these governmental thoroughfares of opportunity and so lighten an apperceived burden upon the welfare state. In other words, Brown had advocated a welfare reorganisation that appeared to mirror Merton's 'governmental avenue' prescription for the cure of functional failure.

Furthermore, this provision of 'opportunity' was seen in the context of an environment of 'amicable' competition. Consequently, Kim Howells, the Labour front bench spokesman for Industry was able to appeal for all "[b]rothers and sisters [to] embrace competition" (Howells, 1996, p 21), while Labour's Economic Policy Commission (1995, p 14) stipulated that "the job of Government is neither to suppress markets nor to surrender to them but to equip people, companies and countries to succeed within them". Put simply, such success was to be secured through the creation of a "partnership between the public and private sectors, with neither squeezing out the other" (Grice and Prescott, 1994, p 1). Social mobility would be a key component in forging this relationship. Retraining would provide the means out of unemployment and its related conditions, while industry would be provided with a new, increasing and highly skilled workforce. The result, it was argued, would be the proliferation of efficient, competitively prosperous companies and workers within the internal and global markets. Nevertheless, this would be a benign situation, as success was envisaged to be available for everyone – and not just for the 'fortunate few'.

'New Deals', old premises

In the light of this predilection towards functionalist ideals, it is entirely consistent for the 'New Deals' put forward by Blair et al to actively promote work-based 'opportunities' for individuals to gain more independence – and responsibility – in their *'escape'* from poverty and dependency. Moreover, a deeper examination into the details that lay behind the 'New Deal' scenario also reveals that these 'deals' are merely continuations of previously tried schemes in authoritarian welfare. They are not 'new' in the respect that they are premised upon Murray's character assassination of the poor. The moral embellishments of Mead and Ellwood remain as guidelines for the proferred treatment of the 'feckless'. Likewise, Etzioni's communitarian rhetoric can be seen to persist while work is viewed as the obligatory passport back into the accepted norms of society.

As in the earlier functionalist approaches, work continues as the means towards social cohesion and aspirational satisfaction since paid work is "the main means of integration". As such it is explicitly seen as the "route to an adequate income, social networks and personal fulfilment". Therefore "[a]ttachment to the labour market ... is the key to breaking the vicious cycle of long-term unemployment and social exclusion" (Levitas, 1996, pp 13-14). Effectively, the New Deal scenario represents a thinly veiled re-dressing of previously implemented American examples in social engineering and sociological debate whereby the "ethic of work provides the financial rationale to get people 'off welfare and into work', and the moral imperative to turn people into better citizens" (Williams, 2004, p 28).

The Department of Social Security's Green Paper *New ambitions for our country: A new contract for welfare* (Government Green Paper, 1998b) constitutes an ideal example of this re-dressing of US themes. As with many of the narratives discussed earlier, the constantly reoccurring themes of 'education/re-education', 'obligation', 'mutual responsibility', 'self-reliance' and the concept of 'workfare' have now become unequivocally entwined in the New Deal idiom of the Labour Party. 'Opportunity' is to be paternalistically enforced upon 'dysfunctional' individuals in a graphic demonstration of the positive exercise of functionalist thought and its associated interpretations of human behaviour. To quote this Green Paper (1998b, ch 3, p 1):

> The Government's aim is to build the welfare state around work. The skills and energies of the workforce are the UK's biggest economic asset. And for both individuals and

families, paid work is the most secure means of averting poverty and dependence.

In order to secure this aim, New Labour's solutions lay in:

- helping people move from welfare to work through the New Deals and Employment Zones;
- developing personalised services to help people into work;
- lowering the barriers to work for those who are able to and want to work;
- and, finally, by making work pay with the introduction of the national minimum wage and reforming the tax–benefit system yet "ensuring that responsibilities and rights are fairly matched" (1998b, ch 3, p 2).

In a self-declared ambition to achieve "nothing less than a change of culture among benefit claimants" (1998b, ch 3, p 2), the first tranche of six New Deals were introduced between 1998 and 1999 in an attempt to steer a variety of non-employed groups through various "'gateways' into the labour market" (Hewitt, 2002, p 192). Using 'carrot and stick' measures (Hewitt, 2002; Driver, 2004) to coerce or encourage individuals into the paid labour market each of the gateways – now condensed into the single 'ONE' gateway through which all claimants must pass (Hewitt, 2002) – began the process of targeting young unemployed people; the long-term unemployed; lone parents; those with a disability, or long-term illness; those who are partners of the unemployed or disabled people; and, finally, people aged 50+ (Hewitt, 2002).

For our purposes, the first three categories are of most significance. The 'deal' for the young, for example, amounts to a supposed choice of four 'opportunities':

- subsidised work with an employer who will receive a job subsidy of up to £60 per week;
- full-time education or training for up to 12 months without the loss of benefit for those without basic education;
- a six-month voluntary sector job;
- or, work on an Environmental Taskforce (Driver, 2004).

Crucially for New Labour, all these options involve training and do not include the fifth option of claiming welfare without working. In addition, the original £2.6 billion investment also included a "£750 grant to employers to provide their New Deal employees with training towards a recognised qualification" (Government Green Paper, 1998, ch 3, pp 3-4).

Similarly, with the long-term unemployed, the government has attempted to "raise skills in the adult population and promote employability" (1998, ch 3, p 4) through an initial investment of £350 million that gives employers a substantial job subsidy of £75 per week, for a period of six months, if they employ those "over the age of 25 who have been out of work for more than two years" (1998, ch 3, p 5). With regard to the New Deal for lone parents, the situation is slightly different. Although participation in the New Deal for lone parents remains voluntary, since April 2002 it has become compulsory for lone parents claiming Income Support to attend work-focused interviews (Millar and Ridge, 2002; Daguerre and Taylor-Gooby, 2004). Even so, despite the voluntary aspect of this particular New Deal, the overarching aim still relates to traditional notions of employment with New Labour setting itself the target of getting 70% of lone parents into the paid labour market (Government Green Paper, 2001). All of which, one might argue, is highly commendable. More so, when one realises that this is only a part of a society-wide package designed to radically alter the way life is conducted in this country.

Appropriately throughout, New Labour sees education as the major platform for the creation of a 'New Britain'. Through the creation of the now defunct 'individual learning accounts', a University for Industry (UfI), and through an improvement of 'excellence in schools' (Government White Paper, 1997; Government Green Paper, 1998a, p 8), the present government aims to equip the nation for the "information and knowledge-based revolution of the twenty-first century" (Government Green Paper, 1998a, p 9). In short, "learning is essential to a strong economy and an inclusive society. In offering a way out of dependency and low expectation, it lies at the heart of the Government's welfare reform" (1998a, p 11). Their key to success is to encourage everyone to innovate and gain with the use of imagination, ingenuity and enterprise. Yet this has not only to happen "in research laboratories, but on the production line, in design studios, in retail outlets, and in providing services" (1998a, pp 9-10). In the words of New Labour, the single, greatest challenge is to link the most productive investment with the best educated and best trained workforces, since "the most effective way of getting and keeping a job will be to have the skills needed by employers" (1998a, p 10). Consequently, to cope – even to prosper – within this new age, we all need to be given new and better skills gleaned from knowledge and understanding (1998a, p 10).

Formally, the individual learning accounts were seen as an integral, but by no means independent, first step towards achieving this goal. In essence they were conceived as saving schemes that, theoretically, would enable varied individuals to be "best placed to choose what and how they want to learn [where] responsibility for investing in learning is shared" (1998a, p 27). These accounts were originally designed to encourage as many people as possible to save and use them. Initially this inducement could take the form of tax incentives or, alternatively, by matching individual contributions with public funding. Ultimately the intention was for a range of financial institutions to offer these accounts in a private partnership with the people, and so alleviate the burden upon government expenditure. So that individuals, and for that matter companies, could make informed decisions on learning and use their learning accounts appropriately, New Labour also proposed to set up special, innovatory centres which would provide advice on the courses individuals need alongside available information on "what their account could buy them and which providers are right for them" (1998a, p 27).

In this respect, the UfI played and still plays a central yet flexible role in the provision of information and education. Under the auspices of the UfI would-be learners are given, on the one hand, the chance to study in easily accessible learning/information centres close to their homes. Indeed as early as September 1997, such centres in Sunderland (one of the original pilot areas) had been set up in "local Training and Enterprise Councils (TECs), libraries, companies, community schools and further education colleges, and a local football club" (Matlay and Hyland, 1999, p 255). On the other, the UfI learner could also take the opportunity to study at home through the Open University-inspired e-learning network, Learndirect, that was officially launched in October 2000 (AoC/UfI, 2001).

Notably, New Labour promotes the UfI as the medium by which priority target areas can be identified in "a private-public partnership" (Government Green Paper, 1998a, p 19) with industry, learning providers and government. Through Learndirect, and its six private 'hub operators' responsible for delivery[1], it is believed that a curriculum addressing an identified shortage of basic skills; information technology expertise; techniques useful for the management of small- and medium-sized businesses; and the specific requirements demanded by industries and services (Government Green Paper, 1998a, p 19) can be effectively conveyed to the appropriate areas concerned. Only in this way, argues

New Labour and its partners, can impetus be given to the task of "addressing the issues of workforce development, increased adult participation and attainment, and raising skills nationwide" (AoC/UfI, 2001, p 4).

With regard to widening participation in further or higher education, proposals and policy implementations for reform have also gathered momentum. According to Watson and Bourne (2001), for instance, there has been a whole plethora of initiatives emanating from New Labour's preliminary Green Paper of 1998. Certainly the recent introduction of a means-tested Educational Maintenance Allowance of up to £30 per week for those living in England and born between 1 September 1987 and 31 August 1988 has greatly enhanced New Labour's desire to promote education beyond the minimum school-leaving age of 16. Nevertheless, three significant changes – primarily aimed at fostering a sense of individual responsibility (through work in the paid labour market) in 'partnership' with governmental responsibility (through subsidised education estimated to cost around £10 billion per year by 2005-06 [Government White Paper, 2003]) – have affected, or will affect, higher education and those attending university.

First, New Labour has abolished student grant awards in favour of student loans – although a new national grant of up to £1,000 per year for students from lower-income families is proposed for 2004 (Government White Paper, 2003). Second, repayment of loans are now collected by the Inland Revenue when working salaries reach the level of £10,000 as opposed to the previous figure of £15,000. Third, it is anticipated that the early expectation for students to contribute up to £1,000 per year towards their own tuition fees (Government Green Paper, 1998a) will, in 2006, be replaced by a Graduate Contribution Scheme giving universities the freedom to set fees ranging from £0 to £3000 (Government White Paper, 2003). Nonetheless, payment will not have to be up front. On the contrary, the new scheme will "link monthly repayments to earnings through the tax system" (2003, para 7.30) once the graduate has secured employment.

In schools, however, proposed changes represent a slightly more recognisable mirror image of New Labour's would-be society at large. Schools would be the primary vehicles by which individuals become equipped to compete in the globally successful 'New' Britain of the future. Indeed, schools are seen to be at the heart of a long-term solution to the perceived ills in the British society of today. 'Opportunity' and the possibilities for personal achievement are, yet again, prominent keys to future development. With this in mind, the government sees education as "'the bedrock' of the programme to modernise and reform the country" (Naidoo and Muschamp, 2002, p 146) through the assertion that education "is the most effective route out of poverty" (Government Annual Report, 1999-2000, cited in Naidoo and Muschamp, 2002, pp 146-7). In sum, the government (Green Paper, 1998a, p 3) argues that to:

> overcome economic and social disadvantage and to make equality of opportunity a reality, we must strive to eliminate, and never excuse, under-achievement in the most deprived parts of our country. Educational attainment encourages aspiration and self-belief in the next generation, and it is through family learning as well as scholarship through formal schooling that success will come.

Starting with 'baseline' assessments for children at the age of four, the present government in its White Paper *Excellence in schools* (1997) advocates that by 2002 it will have created a nationwide improvement in education at all levels. It is argued that improvement will be achieved by 'streaming' every pupil according to ability. Confronted with league tables of achievement, pupils, teachers, schools and Local Education Authorities (LEAs) will be set targets that they have to either attain or maintain. With the availability of training and retraining teachers will be subsequently judged solely upon their ability, while headteachers would be subject to acquiring newly recognised qualifications for the job. For New Labour, better teachers mean better schools and pupils. Therefore failure to improve will not be tolerated. Persistently inadequate teachers will be dismissed. Continually underachieving schools will be closed. Inept LEAs will be deprived of their powers and replaced by central control. Overall, the government's "aim is excellence for everyone [with a] commitment to zero tolerance of underperformance" (Government White Paper, 1997, p 12).

In relation to the curriculum, emphasis is placed upon supplying industry with the skills it needs to succeed in the global economy. At primary school level, literacy and numeracy will take priority in the belief that children can only make a success of their lives if "they can read and write fluently, handle numbers confidently, and concentrate on their work" (Government White Paper, 1997, p 15). Beyond primary level, New Labour concentrate their efforts on "Modernising the comprehensive principle" (1997, p 37). Although talk is of developing all the diverse talents of the pupils, there is a definite slant towards vocational skills as a preparatory basis for adult life. Excellence for everyone is seen to be attainable through a system that replaces the loss of high-skilled apprenticeships and, as such, allows "individuals to mature and develop" (1997, p 37) prior to joining the workforce.

All of this entails a greater emphasis upon the more vocationally oriented GNVQs and school–business links (Government White Paper, 1997, p 61) as opposed to the more academic A-levels. Similarly, in a direct attempt to counter immediate skill shortages, it is intended that the curriculum of individual schools should be tailored to fit the needs of the surrounding areas through the creation of Education Action Zones (EAZs), which were initially launched in six urban areas by the Prime Minister and David Blunkett in March 1999 (Naidoo and Muschamp, 2002). Indeed, two successive expansions have meant that these 'zones' covered 58 authority areas by the start of 2001 (DfEE, 2001) while in August of the same year, the establishment of a further 23 smaller EAZs as part of the Excellence in Cities programme brought the total of operational 'zones' up to 81 (Naidoo and Muschamp, 2002).

By way of further reinforcement, it is planned that this shift towards industry in the curriculum will soon be supplemented with an improved network of information and communications technology. In the long term, schools will not only be linked to a 'National Grid' for learning but will also be part of "an extensive network of specialist schools benefiting neighbouring schools and the local community" (Government White Paper, 1997, p 44). In sum, this is New Labour's drive for yet another public–private partnership, a partnership in which responsibility for teaching, policy direction, educational support and costs would be benignly shared by government, business and the families of the community.

Finally, this concept of a partnership for success returns us back to the workplace. New Labour envisage a transformation in industrial relations through a conciliatory "programme to replace the notion of conflict between employers and employees with the promotion of partnership" (Blair, quoted in Government White Paper, 1998, p 3). With the Employment Relations Act (1999), New Labour have rhetorically sought to enhance, if not restore, collective rights (Novitz and Skidmore, 2001) through greater trade union recognition in the workplace and the legislative promise that *Fairness at work* (Government White Paper, 1998) will evolve out of a cultural change in working relationships. Competitiveness and fairness are seen to go hand in hand since efficiency and fairness can only be secured through the employability and flexibility of the workforce (1998, p 14). However, to support this employability and flexibility, New Labour believes they need "a labour market culture and a legislative framework which together promote economic growth, enhance competitiveness, encourage entrepreneurship and foster job creation" (1998, p 14). Indeed, such a change in the "culture of labour relations" (Novitz and Skidmore, 2001, p 1) is only deemed to be possible with the establishment of minimum standards of employment below which no individual in work is allowed to fall. Not only do these standards include the previously mentioned minimum wage, but they also include new maternity and paternity concessions alongside a renewed commitment to the maintenance of health and safety standards at work. Nevertheless, in offering these new rights, New Labour demands "that employees in return accept their responsibilities to cooperate with employers" (Government White Paper, 1998, p 14).

In keeping with this balancing of rights with responsibility, New Labour advocate that the increases in individual and union rights to recognition and representation have to be tempered with formalised procedures of negotiation. Crucially, the Employment Relations Act (1999) places the onus firmly upon mutuality by encouraging "unions and employers to voluntarily agree to recognition procedures [and stressing] that statutory procedures [only] apply 'when unions and employers are unable to reach agreement voluntarily'" (Gall and McKay, 2001, p 95). Consequently, trade unions are advised to focus "more strongly on working with management to develop a flexible, skilled and motivated workforce. Trade unions can be a force for fair treatment, and a means of driving towards innovation and partnerships" (Government White Paper, 1998, p 22). Overall, New Labour believes that the extent of trade union growth has to be dependent upon the ability of trade unions to convince employers and employees of their value. It has to be based on "how much help [trade unions] can bring to the success of an enterprise for employers, and how much active support they can offer employees" (1998, p 23). Only through this actively reciprocal relationship can 'fairness at work' be achieved. Only in this way, so the argument goes, can both the employer and employee survive and flourish in the global markets of today.

All of which combine to make a very comprehensive package indeed. Each of the New Deals mentioned reinforces the others. When taken as a whole we can now see a more tangible model of how New Labour is converting their pre-1997 thoughts into actual policy. In all areas of society, functionalist trains of thought predominate. A social hierarchy – even in schools – provides the framework in which individual aspiration can be pursued and attained. Competition, especially that engendered from the market, is taken as a force to encourage both personal motivation and feelings of achievement. In the school, workplace and the community success with its associated rewards represents the ultimate goal for everyone. This is the source of personal satisfaction, whereas 'opportunity', in the forms of 'workfare', education and justice at work is to be secured by governmental directives. In this way, Labour in government envisage an almost universal improvement of present-day social ills. Pathways of 'opportunity' in the market context are the keys to the eradication of social exclusion. They are the keys to future success for all.

Blair's communitarianisms and support for the family

On reflection, it is apparent that New Labour's global image of a partnership between the state, employers and employees (or volunteers) represents a fusion of the respective stances taken by Murray, Mead and Ellwood. Through the New Deals, New Labour is attempting to reassert both the notion of responsibility and, of course, attempting to prescribe a cure for the apparently 'work-shy' and socially disruptive members of the so-called 'underclass'. From the outset, however, this policy direction again points back to New Labour's affinity to Giddens. Indeed, Tony Blair (2003, p 28) reiterates the thoughts of Giddens when he suggests that the 'third way':

> stands for a modernised social democracy, passionate in its commitment to social justice and the goals of the centre left, but flexible, innovative and forward-looking in the means to achieve them. It is founded on the values [of] democracy, liberty, justice, mutual obligation and internationalism. But it is a 'third way' because it moves decisively beyond an Old Left preoccupied by state control, high taxation and producer interests; and a New Right treating public investment, and often the very notions of 'society' and collective endeavour, as evils to be undone.

There is little doubt here that Blair and Giddens share the same sentiments. Likewise, such a declaration also strikes a familiar chord with the thoughts of Etzioni that were expressed in Chapter Three.

Nevertheless, a more detailed exposition of what can now be called 'Blair's communitarianisms' would significantly enhance the strength of the connections described so far. By doing so, this closer examination will also provide the starting point from which Chapter Seven can begin to raise some tentative concerns about the policies New Labour has chosen to implement. But first, it is necessary to briefly recall the overarching stance of Etzioni. In truth, the communitarianism of Etzioni can be summarised by five basic characteristics. First, Chapter Three has shown that this form of communitarianism places most of its emphasis on one moral community at the expense of plurality and diversity. Second, it has been revealed that there is a prominent desire to return to a traditional and nostalgic past. The third aspect of Etzioni's communitarianism reflects a neglect to consider hierarchical power structures while the fourth attribute significantly contributes to a sustained critique of personal rights. With respect to the fifth and final facet, it is generally recognised that this particular brand of communitarianism represents a moralistic rallying call for the return to traditional family forms in order to combat perceived social ills and dysfunctionality (see Hughes and Little, 1998; Heron and Dwyer, 1999; Prideaux, 2002, 2004).

Arguably, the policies, rhetoric and interpretations of New Labour, like those of Giddens, do not appear to significantly differ from those of Etzioni. On a methodological level, for example, it is clear that New Labour's approach to the problems facing British society is remarkably reminiscent of Etzioni's analysis of the US in the 1980s and 1990s. In this respect, Driver and Martell (1997) point out that New Labour tends to restrict its analysis to a comparison of polar opposites. Pluralist approaches are set against conformist; more conditional against less conditional; progressive against conservative; prescriptive against voluntary; moral against socioeconomic; and individual against corporate. As with Etzioni's (and indeed Giddens') style of investigation, the resultant recommendations or solutions to perceived problems invariably become defined by the chosen *Gemeinschaft/Gesellschaft* images attached. The depiction of a growing, menacing 'underclass', for instance, deliberately suggests that individual responsibility is the answer to welfare dependency. Likewise, the warm image of a work-centred communal morality easily outshines the loneliness of hedonistic individuality. Significantly, though, the approach of New Labour can be seen to emulate Etzioni's negligence in that it also fails to account for the possible conflicts and contradictions that the system of capitalism may still pose.

With specific regard to rhetoric and policy direction comparisons between communitarianism and New Labour are even clearer. Markedly, Prideaux (2001) and Heron (2001) independently point to the original but persisting concept of 'stakeholding' and its emphasis on individuals taking an active 'stake' in a society or community. Powell et al (2001) explore the connection with Etzioni through New Labour's *zeitgeist* of a 'partnership' between people, communities and government. Deacon (2002) looks at the moral 'judgementalism' of Etzioni and New Labour (see also Deacon and Mann, 1997, 1999; Driver and Martell, 2002), whereas Levitas (1998), as we have previously noted, points to the characteristic centrality that both give to the 'family' and 'community' as theatres for learning and social control. All reinforce Driver and Martell's (1998, p 29) observation that if communitarianism "is New Labour's answer to Thatcherism; so too is it Blair's rebuff to Old Labour. Community will restore the moral balance to society by setting out duties and obligations as well as rights".

Basically, it is the communitarian emphasis upon family, community, social discipline, obligation and responsibility – as opposed to an indiscriminate conferral of rights – that lies behind New Labour's search for a 'third way' that would go 'beyond Left and Right' (Giddens, 1994). Besides the repeated references to the term 'community', Etzionian influences permeate New Labour's policy drive to reaffirm a sense of community. To reiterate, there is little doubt that New Labour want to reinvigorate the institution of the family (Barlow and Duncan, 1999; Fox Harding, 2000; Driver and Martell, 2002) yet maintain market relations by giving primacy to paid work (Levitas, 1998). Without doubt also, its moral evaluation of the 'irresponsible' welfare claimant has produced a rationale designed to provoke a change of 'culture' (Deacon and Mann, 1997, 1999; Government Green Paper, 1998b; Deacon, 2002). In short, New Labour envisages that its most fundamental task is to instil a sense of responsibility through the welfare principle of 'conditionality' (Dwyer, 1998, 2000a, 2000b, 2002; Heron and Dwyer, 1999).

Given this, it now becomes logical and consistent for New Labour to expand the continued existence of the uncompromising Child Support Agency (CSA). Similarly, the introduction of the Working Families Tax Credit (WFTC), as part of a National Childcare Strategy, also adheres to this communitarian logic. Equally, these measures have a judgemental approach. All include notions of obligation and behavioural change. And all signify the importance New Labour attaches to the traditional role of the family.

With WFTC, the communitarian associations are particularly obvious. Work is inextricably entwined with conceptions of the family. Although WFTC attempts to give better in-work benefits to both lone-parent and two-parent families with children in which there is an adult in full-time (16+ hours) low-paid employment (Dean and

Shah, 2002), there is the real possibility of a rather perverse consequence. By enabling men with limited earning power to support a non-working wife, WFTC could help "re-establish the male breadwinner model among certain low-income households" (Dean, 2002, p 6). Etzioni would not be too disturbed by such a trend. Nor, one suspects, would New Labour, even though their declared aim in this area is to promote the idea that all should be able to combine paid work and family life.

New Labour's plans for the CSA strengthen this suspicion. In keeping faith with the founding Conservative principle that "no father should be able to escape from his responsibility" (Margaret Thatcher, quoted in Timmins, 1996, p 452), the CSA still maintains its presence under New Labour. Moreover, despite the failures of this agency New Labour are determined to link its activities with an effort to get lone parents on benefit back to work through the relevant New Deal scheme on offer. This in itself does not appear to question the family structure. Neither does it suggest that women should stay at home. However, the original and little heard of consultation proposal for a male mentoring scheme in the Sure Start element of the *New Deal for communities* (Home Office, 1998) betrays their thinking. The whole idea of a male mentor for a male child undermines the responsibility of a single mother. It suggests a deep mistrust of a single mother's ability to cope alone. Instead, emphasis is placed on paid work and the inevitable involvement of others undertaking the necessary childcaring duties.

Likewise in a follow-up document, New Labour's intention to "improve couples' decision making about getting married, and to enhance services which prevent marriage breakdown" (Driver and Martell, 2002, p 51) substantiates these misgivings further. In spite of Driver and Martell's belief that the document *Supporting families: Summary of responses to the consultation document* (Home Office, 1999a) has a largely pragmatic view on family forms, the proposals given send a rather different message. True to maintaining the ideal of traditional family forms, the proposals recommend:

> an increased role for registrars in marriage guidance; a statement of the rights and responsibilities of marriage and the ceremony; the restructuring of marriage counselling to place greater stress on saving marriages; and funding for marriage advice centres. (Driver and Martell, 2002, p 51)

The wistful tone, content and intent of the document could easily have come from Etzioni's review of relationships in 1950s' America, especially in the light of Etzioni's (1995) comments on what he sees as a 'parenting deficit'.

Structural-functionalism unearthed: a summation

Effectively, the cases discussed in this chapter have been illustrative of the functionalist tendencies that inform aspects of New Labour's social policy. Certainly, the discussion of the influence exerted by Giddens and Etzioni has revealed that New Labour sees 'work', the 'family' (almost in a traditional sense), 'community' and 'schooling' as the bedrock for social development (Prideaux, 2004). As part of a virtuous cycle, families are primarily seen as institutions of social control and social welfare. They are "where the difference between right and wrong is learned, and where a sense of mutual obligation is founded and practised" (Mandelson and Liddle, 1996, p 125) and it is "largely from family discipline that social discipline and a sense of responsibility is learned" (Blair, 1994a, p 90).

In support, education at school, work and in wider society provides more discipline and a further reinforcement of the basic values taught in the family. Finally (in a chronological sense), work and participation in the market is seen to generate more responsibility and enable self-sufficiency for the future. In so doing, work thus stimulates the economy, encourages a greater moral sensibility, creates a stronger feeling of belonging and, ultimately, stimulates the growth of a comforting and supportive community which, for New Labour, "is not some piece of nostalgia [since community] means what we share, it means working together" (Blair, 1996, p 64). In this way, the cycle of virtuosity perpetuates as the community complements familial relations.

This book's concluding chapter takes a different stance to that of the early functionalists and New Labour. The chapter does not hold with the characteristic view that capitalism is a quintessentially benign social system devoid of conflict and corruption. On the contrary, conflict and contradiction are deemed to be inherent to the dynamic of capitalism. Consequently, Chapter Seven promotes an alternative evaluation of the possible areas of tension and friction that New Labour's social policies may yet face in the highly competitive environment of the laissez-faire market system.

Note

[1] The six organisations responsible for the delivery of Learndirect in nine industrial sectors are: ASSA Training and Learning Ltd (in the sectors for automotive components, automotive skills, science and engineering, audio-

visual communications); CITB Construction Skills (construction); Knowledge Base UK Limited (sports and recreation); NWLCC Limited (logistics); and Manchester Enterprises (process manufacturing industries) (Ufl/Learndirect, 2003).

SEVEN

Conclusion

Functionalism and New Labour

Integral to the whole of this work has been the fundamental premise that New Labour essentially holds a benign view of capitalism. Throughout, it has become apparent such a viewpoint resembles many of the social deliberations surrounding the attempts of structural-functionalist thinkers to legitimise US socioeconomic conditions of the 1940s, 1950s and 1960s. Thus, the book began from the standpoint that New Labour, as with the likes of Talcott Parsons and his devotees, primarily interprets capitalist relations in a manner that depicts "an optimistic and voluntaristic view of social reality" (Robertson and Turner, 1991, p 9).

As a result, a central concern has been that structural-functionalism has managed – despite any possibilities of conflict, acquiescence and dominance – to provide a significant theoretical guide to the policy direction undertaken by New Labour. Of critical importance here, is Chapter Five's inversion of the reasoning as to why ideas become policy. Indeed, such an inversion helped to explain why the inclusion of what initially seem to be non-functionalist ideas (such as those purported by Murray in 1984) have been included in the overall discussion. As with Mann and Roseneil's (1994) belief that an idea has to appeal to a number of different constituencies for it to become successful, then, for functionalism to persist, it was suggested that the reverse also has to be held true. In other words, a number of apparently different and diversified ideas have to complement and substantiate the overarching framework of functionalism. On this basis, an integral proposition of the book was that the functionalism of New Labour is able to flourish because of the fact that complementary debates such as those surrounding the 'underclass' and the aforementioned drive to manage individual behaviour (Chapter Five), society (Chapter Three) and the economy in general have effectively underpinned a Parsonian-cum-Etzionian view of society.

With this complicated scenario in mind, the focus of Chapter Two was upon early functionalist constructions of society. In particular, attention focused on the essential factors that Parsons (1949, 1966, 1967), Merton (1968) and Davis and Moore (1967) attributed to social cohesion. Primarily these deliberations, and those of Parsons in particular, reflected the beginning of a US inspired hegemony that eventually fuelled a global period of American economic, military and cultural domination (Kilminster, 1998). By concentrating upon these highly influential sociological thinkers, Chapter Two provided a stable platform from which an effective understanding of functionalism could be gleaned and applied throughout the rest of the book. To reiterate, these American structural-functionalists saw the US version of capitalism as the ideal form of social relations. It was a benign social pyramid of opportunity that, through motivational competition and the free-market economy, satiated the aspiration of responsible hard-working individuals and duly rewarded them for their endeavours.

Organisational theory, new communitarianism and the 'dysfunctional' individual

After having established a working definition of functionalism, Chapter Three demonstrated how the early sociological leanings of Amitai Etzioni and, to a lesser extent, those of Philip Selznick have influenced their thoughts on the future development of society as a whole. Etzioni was pivotal to making the link between New Labour and structural-functionalism, not least because there has been little doubt over the deep influence that Etzioni and his communitarian movement have exerted on Blair and New Labour (Deacon and Mann, 1997, 1999; Driver and Martell, 1998, 2002; Heron, 2001; Powell et al, 2001; Prideaux, 2001, 2004; Deacon, 2002). In this respect, the book has consistently shown that shared concerns relating to notions of 'community', 'partnership' and the composition of what can be seen as an 'ideal' family form have significantly underpinned the social deliberations of both New Labour and Etzioni.

Taken in this context, Chapter Three specifically concentrated upon how organisational studies throughout the 1960s and 1970s were fundamentally restricted to the search for economic efficiency within the laissez-faire market environment (see Allen, 1975). Surprisingly, this is not a charge that has been rigorously applied to the communitarian bibles of *The spirit of community* (Etzioni, 1995), *The new golden rule* (Etzioni, 1997) and *The essential communitarian reader* (Etzioni, 1998). Yet, by levelling this charge – and by providing a more detailed examination of Etzioni's applied methodology – the chapter was able to fully reveal the extent to which communitarians such as

Etzioni have relied upon their functionalist origins. In this way, the chapter was able to expose the underlying limitations of these societal projections (Prideaux, 2002). In particular, it was argued that Etzioni has taken the methodological influence of structural-functionalism and Parsons beyond the realms of its organisational offshoot and forged it into a prescriptive attempt at a cure for the perceived ills of modern society. As a result, it was argued that Etzioni had become guilty of trying to impose his own US version of community upon the rest of the Western world. And given the widely recognised influence that Etzioni has exerted upon New Labour, this myopic viewpoint thus provided the rest of the book with the argument that New Labour has adopted a rather narrow perspective upon which to build many of its social policies.

The introduction of the 'so-called' communitarian John Macmurray (Rentoul, 1997; Driver and Martell, 1998; Levitas, 1998; Hale, 2002) in Chapter Four was both demonstrative and practical. Demonstrative in the sense that it was Blair himself (in Rentoul, 1997, p 42; in Conford, 1996, p 9) who declared Macmurray to be an influence, yet paradoxically has not acknowledged Macmurray's anti-communitarian, anti-capitalist and anti-functionalist stance. Practical in that the works of Macmurray provide a direct contrast to those of Etzioni (hence the final comparison of the two at the end of the chapter). Practical, also, in that the inclusion of Macmurray helped cement the connections between New Labour and functionalism. As the book has demonstrated in later chapters, the lack of any true and detailed recourse by either Blair or New Labour to the work of Macmurray only served to further emphasise the reliance placed on Etzioni's neoconservatism as opposed to the more libertarian based socialism of Macmurray.

Chapter Five expanded upon the notion of ideas having to appeal to different constituencies by bringing the beliefs of the New Right into the debate. To be more accurate, this chapter introduced the pragmatic compatibility of specifically 'right-wing' ideas to the fundamental standpoint of New Labour. Consequently, arguments presented by the overtly libertarian Charles Murray (1984, 1986a, 1986b, 1996a, 1996b) became central to this work. Indeed, their inclusion in the chapter not only helped to fully demonstrate the importation of American ideas into the British political arena, but they also significantly helped to reinforce the functionalism behind New Labour's policy statements described in Chapter Six.

After all, argued Chapter Five, Murray's belief that the members of the so-called 'underclass' deliberately led an immoral, crime-oriented lifestyle simply underlined their rational rejection of the accepted norms of society. Therefore, Murray's recommended solution to withdraw welfare payments to these individuals reflected a move to force them back into the realms of social normality. Implicitly, Murray's depiction of the 'underclass' ventured that the good 'citizens' of this world had to work hard, be honest and had to come from a 'stable' family background. In plain English, they must follow the functionally prescribed moral norms of society: it is not acceptable for individuals to be dysfunctional. In this latter respect, of course, it was the final inclusion of the work of Lawrence Mead (1986, 1987, 1988, 1991), who specifically related to 'dysfunctional' individuals and families, that provided a direct route to accommodate Murray's deliberations on the 'underclass' firmly within the functionality hypothesis as a whole.

Taking the 'third way' towards 'partnership'

In Chapter Six, the process of unravelling some of the main policy manifestations of New Labour's functionalism began. Initially, this chapter discussed Anthony Giddens' (1994, 1998, 2000, 2003) complementary notions of the 'third way' and how it reflected a remarkable similarity to the communitarian beliefs of Etzioni. Moreover, given the acknowledged influence that Giddens has been able to exert upon New Labour during his time as director of the London School of Economics, the chapter was able to introduce the reasoning behind the work-based New Deal schemes and subsequently place them within the context of Blair's communitarianisms. Taken in conjunction with Chapters Two and Three, these connections also helped to further cement the functionalist basis for New Labour's social policies. In this respect, it was shown that a prominent feature of New Labour's functionalism is the tendency to give primacy to the concept of 'equality of opportunity' in an attempt to counter perceived social ills. 'Equality of opportunity', it was argued, represents the means by which New Labour could reassert the value of paid work and so stimulate a renewed sense of community.

Unmistakably, Chapter Six demonstrated that the promotion of 'equality of opportunity', as opposed to an 'equality of outcome', represents a complete embodiment of the Etzionian vision of responsible citizens acting to preserve their stake in society yet striving to promote the vision of a moral commonwealth (Selznick, 1994). Furthermore, it was also pointed out that the association with the New Deal re-emphasises the influence of Mead and, to a lesser extent, Murray, in that irresponsible individuals have to be forced back into the realms of responsibility through the application of welfare-to-work principles. In sum, the chapter described how New Labour's preconceived visions of individual responsibility, self-reliance and moral duty to the community have become inextricably entwined with the key element of a New Deal 'partnership' between the government (as providers and administrators of 'opportunities'), the private sector (as employers of New Deal participants) and the individual (taking the responsible step of accepting the opportunity of work in the paid labour market) to form a benign interpretation of both capitalism and society as a whole.

Inherent contradictions and tensions

Up to now, the main purpose of the book has been to explore the connections between the social deliberations of New Labour and the sociology underpinning functionalism, organisational theory and the US-inspired revival of communitarianism. In so doing, it has gradually become apparent that a number of different tensions have been simmering beneath the surface of the social prescriptions advocated and deployed. With regard to New Labour's economic stance, for instance, it is evident New Labour demonstrates a munificence towards capitalism and its entrepreneurs that is strikingly similar to the attitudes of the functionalist thinkers discussed in this book. In this respect, Clarke (2004) helps the book to further explore the wisdom of this benign outlook by revealing some of the profound areas of friction that are being generated by such an approach.

Without directly referring to functionalism or Parsons in the manner of this work, Clarke (2004, p 30) compatibly argues that the US-driven, neoliberal globalisation process of today should be viewed as a mobile, 'anglophone West' strategy which not only "attempts to install itself as the only, the necessary and the most desirable way [but also] attempts to 'hegemonise' supra-national institutions". In relation to Britain, contends Clarke, it is a strategy that has demonstrated its mobility by consistently attempting to form and re-form alliances and blocs in order to obtain dominance through the demobilisation of alternative possibilities. Accordingly, neoliberalism (in the more benevolent guise of New Labour's functionalism) has provided an active challenge to public interest with its concerted effort to simultaneously dissolve the public realm and supplant it with the rule of private interests coordinated by the 'free market'. Thus for Clarke (2004, p 31), neoliberalism has insisted that:

the 'monopoly providers' of public services be replaced by efficient suppliers disciplined by the competitive realities of the market. It has disintegrated conceptions of the public as a collective identity, attempting to substitute individualised and economised identities as taxpayers and consumers.

As the book has touched upon on a number of occasions (see Chapter Two in particular and Chapter Six by implication), integral to this challenge to public interests is neoliberalism's insistence that primacy has to be given to the private. Yet, as Clarke demonstrates, the meaning and application of the 'private' in neoliberal terms is variable. In one sense, the 'private' designates the market as a vehicle of private interests and exchange. Nevertheless, 'private' in this context represents both the interests of the abstract individual (customarily referred to as the 'rational economic man') and the competitive corporation that is treated as a human entity in its own right. Indeed, through this personification, each type of individual (real or anthropomorphised) suffers the heavy burden of "taxation, the excesses of regulation, the interference with their freedom and [the] shackling of [their] 'entrepreneurial spirit' by big government" (Clarke, 2004, p 31).

In another sense, neoliberal usage of the word 'private' is also a point of reference for the familial/domestic sphere. The 'rational economic man' is also a 'family man' aspiring to achieve his own (sic) interests and those of his immediate family (Clarke, 2004). As Kingfisher (2002, cited in Clarke, 2004, p 32) points out, this not only reflects an ingrained gender bias but also creates a situation whereby 'independence' and 'self-sufficiency' become inextricably entwined to the extent that:

> 'independence' is displayed in the public realm, while 'dependence' is sequestered to the private sphere ... the public, civil society generated by means of the social contract is predicated on the simultaneous generation of a private sphere, into which is jettisoned all that is not amenable to contract.

Certainly, New Labour is of the same mindset to that of the neoliberal strategy. As Chapter Six of this book has shown, New Labour sees economic efficiency as an integral, interwoven aspect of both social cohesion and social morality (Duncan, 2000). Like Etzioni's deliberations in Chapter Three, New Labour envisage a 'moral efficiency' tantamount to a neoliberal 'self-sufficiency' that arises out of a reinvigorated sense of community within which each person has a stake in its future and "each person accepts responsibility to respond, to work to improve themselves" (Blair, 1996, p 64).

Consequently, any so-called 'dysfunctional' or 'insufficiently capable' individuals and families who do not behave in the 'appropriate way' have to be encouraged or cajoled back into the designated parameters of self and individual 'responsibility'. When taken in conjunction with New Labour's undoubted promotion of the paid labour market as the prescriptive cure for 'irresponsibility', this immediately indicates that New Labour purport a vision of individuals who exemplify the aforementioned 'rational economic man'. Clearly, from the discussions undertaken in Chapters Five and Six, people are believed to take individualistic and cost–benefit type decisions about how to maximise their own gain and, of course, that of their families. As a result, it is believed that the social behaviour of non-conforming individuals can be modified through changes in the financial and legal structure of costs and benefits (Duncan, 2000). Hence, the previously recounted attempt by New Labour "to build the welfare state around work" (Government Green Paper, 1998b, ch 3, p 1) in order to achieve "nothing less than a change of culture among benefit claimants" (1998b, ch 3, p 2).

Unquestionably, this materialistic interpretation is at odds with Macmurray's relational interpretation described in Chapter Four. Moreover, it is a viewpoint that is at odds with many aspects of contemporary life. Almost as an echo of Macmurray, for example, Mason (2004) points out that the decision making process goes beyond the narrow preconceptions of New Labour. Through semi-structured interviews with 57 people currently living in two cities in the north of England, Mason found that people decided where to live through a process of negotiation (whether it be explicit or otherwise) with others. Of pivotal importance to the interviewees were considerations over kinship, proximity and distance. How could a move be legitimised in both one's own eyes and in those of significant others? How would practical support for oneself and other kin be affected? How (if at all) can supportive kin relationships be maintained or afforded and how willing would those concerned be to continue relations over a distance? Such deliberation indicates that decisions are arrived at through interaction. Interaction appears to shape what can and cannot be done. In essence, it is not rational-economic issues alone that provide guidance over life choices.

From this standpoint, it is apparent that New Labour is making false assumptions about human agency, behaviour, rationality and morality. In so doing, New Labour is trying to impose its own blueprint for responsible behaviour at the expense of those who, possibly for good reason, behave in a different manner. Duncan (2000), for instance, underlines this point by turning attention back to New Labour's attitude towards lone motherhood. According to recent research (Duncan and Edwards, 1999; Standing, 1999; Van Drenth et al, 1999), he argues:

> practically all lone mothers see their moral and practical responsibility for their children as their primary duty and that for many (although not all) this responsibility to be a 'good mother' is seen as largely incompatible with significant paid work. (Duncan, 2000, p 5)

Therefore, New Labour's prescriptive insistence upon lone parents attending interviews with job advisors (Home Office, 1998) is largely an irrelevance – if not a direct threat – to the moral rationality of these individuals. To reiterate, it is not solely a question of paid work reflecting moral responsibility. Under these circumstances, to enforce participation in the paid labour market may exacerbate rather than alleviate the tensions and problems facing lone parents, especially if the parent believes they are neglecting their child or children by leaving them (in the care of others) to go to work elsewhere.

Removing social responsibility from the public sphere

Implicitly, this discussion reflects a second, more pervasive, form of privatisation that has significantly shifted 'social responsibilities' "from the public sphere (where they formed part of the business of government) to the *private sphere* (where they become matters of individual, familial or household concern)" (Clarke, 2004, p 33). Moreover, with the addition of the principle of conditionality that underpins the current New Deal schemes in Britain, the transition to the private has been firmly secured. As Williams (2001, cited in Clarke, 2004, p 33) aptly put it:

> the shift to meaner and more conditional forms of income support 'privatises' the tasks of 'getting by': from personal investment calculations and risks (eg in pensions); to new forms of family economy (multiple wage-earning); and to

indebtedness, loan sharking, and illicit sources of income as means of filling the gap.

In relation to this particular work, the observations of Williams point to four significant areas of probable tension and friction. The first, and most prominent in this extract, relates to the conflict between government use of the prescriptive condition of participation in the paid labour market (as a means to avoid the 'underclass' spiral of immorality, crime and fraudulent benefit claims described in Chapter Five of this book) and the counteracting possibility that individuals may be left with no alternative but to obtain supplementary forms of income in alternative, if not dishonest, ways. In the UK today, it is true that the minimum wage, first introduced in 1999, has set a bottom limit to low-waged labour. Nonetheless, Duncan (2002) argues that the introduction of a minimum wage level has not fully overcome the need to find alternative sources of income. It fails, he continues, because the rate set is deliberately pitched at a low level so that wage levels generally do not interfere with the 'flexibility' industry is perceived to require in a globally competitive free market.

Indeed, this leads to the second area of tension in that continued gendered inequality is, and has been for some time, crucial to Britain's attempt to remain economically competitive through the utilisation of a predominantly female section of the labour force who tend to be low-paid, part time and have a minimum of employment rights (Perrons, 1999; Bagihole and Byrne, 2000; Duncan, 2002). Likewise, this gendered inequality is exacerbated by a third tension embedded within conditional, more frugal forms of welfare and the resultant privatisation of responsibility. Consistent with the cost-conscious concerns that have driven the transfer of welfare to the 'private' is a concomitant transmission of costs from public resources to household resources (Clarke, 2004). Worryingly, this dimension of privatisation assumes the predominance of stable nuclear families based upon a gendered division of domestic, caring labour. As a result, the "conception of infinitely elastic female labour continues to underpin such privatisation" (Clarke, 2004, p 33), despite the increased involvement of women in the paid labour market.

As with Dean's (2002) observation of the perverse consequences of Working Families Tax Credit (WFTC) (see Chapter Six), this gendered inequality directly contradicts Giddens' (1998, 2000) recounted calls (again, see Chapter Six of this book) for government to 'democratise' the family through gender equality, mutual rights and responsibilities and an increased emphasis upon co-parenting. Similarly, continued gendered inequality rests uneasily with Giddens' broader plea to 'democratise democracy' and the government's "liberal, progressive agenda" (Driver and Martell, 2002, p 53) to support women with children in the paid labour market through a childcare allowance in WFTC and the National Childcare Strategy to provide free nursery places for three to four year olds (Driver and Martell, 2002; see also McLaughlin et al, 2001). Succinctly, Kittay (2001) observes that, for new communitarians and – by implication of the arguments set out in Chapters Three and Six of this book – for New Labour, primacy is still accorded to 'traditional' family forms. As a result, "a woman with very young children has only two respectable ways of obtaining income: through a husband or through employment" (Kittay, 2001, p 53).

To compound issues, it has been noted throughout the book that socially approved ways of obtaining income (particularly through 'responsible' participation in the paid labour market) are now an integral part of New Labour's deliberations on acquiring the rights of citizenship (see also Levitas, 2001; Lister, 2001; Dwyer, 2002, 2004; Craig, 2004). Frequently, women undertaking the unpaid caring role (as is so often the case with gendered inequality) are made vulnerable by their likely dependency on either benefits or a significant other. Consequently, women 'carers' are put in the invidious position of being susceptible to poverty, on the one hand, and having to forgo full social citizenship on the other. Certainly, such tensions between New Labour's professed objectives and actual outcomes imitate many of the problems inherent in communitarian thought. Like Etzioni, New Labour rhetorically envisages a potential society of equals capable of full participation in the communal society of tomorrow. Yet, as Williams' (2001) extract intimated earlier, this seriously neglects those:

> persons whose dependency is the result of inevitable conditions related to age, ability, and health [and] are thereby excluded from consideration except as the quasi-property interest of independent equals. Furthermore, the contributions of those labors devoted to caring for dependents become invisible. (Kittay, 2001, p 529)

Kittay's specific references to age, ability and health in this extract neatly turns attention back to Williams' allusion to the tasks of 'getting by' or, by implication, not 'getting by' and the possibility of social exclusion as a consequence. In this respect, a fourth area of tension or friction can be gleaned from New Labour's benign, 'work-first' (Dean, 2003), money/income-centred approach to perceived social problems.

As the following section of this conclusion demonstrates, this is especially true of the prevalent notions of social citizenship and the associated concept of community being used by government today.

Old age, social citizenship and the exclusive community

In its broadest sense, social citizenship is seen "in terms of the ability to access the range of resources and conditions promoting social well-being" (Ackers and Dwyer, 2002, p 14). Clearly, this is not confined to participation in the paid labour market and, as such, helps to highlight the limitations of New Labour's blinkered approach. Indeed, Craig (2004) expands upon Ackers and Dwyer's position by citing Dean and Melrose's (1999) assertion that concepts of citizenship may "do more than simply leave social differences out of account, they may actively reinforce the position of men over women and of majority over minority ethnic groups" (Dean and Melrose, 1999, in Craig, 2004, p 97). The same, continues Craig, could also be said of the circumstances in which some individuals find themselves during the age of retirement.

Of critical importance here, is Craig's overarching conclusion that 'getting by' is completely inadequate, whereas financial remuneration represents only a partial solution to a more general set of problematic circumstances. Research (see Cohen et al, 1990; Sadiq-Sangster, 1991; Kempson, 1996; Gordon and Pantazis, 1997; Parker, 2000), Craig argues (2004, p 99), has effectively demonstrated how low income and low 'take-up' of such benefits has prevented many older people from obtaining goods and services "which most in UK society regarded as meeting essential needs". As a direct consequence, many of those in retirement are prevented from enjoying the rewards of social citizenship in its widest terms.

When drawing upon the findings of a qualitative study undertaken elsewhere, Craig points out that, prior to any successful claims for additional means-tested retirement benefits, the majority of older people complained that they had been unable to manage financially. Of those that could, it became a question of 'cutting your cloth to suit', careful budgeting and "having to make painful financial decisions such as cashing in an endowment policy early" (Craig, 2004, p 102). Generally, informs Craig, the overall consequence of this insecurity was to undermine feelings of self-worth and well-being. Several, it was noted (Craig, 2004, p 103), spoke of isolation and loneliness, while many also spoke "of the limits placed on their ability to be mobile or to attend social events and the effects this had on the extent of their social participation".

After successful claims for means-tested benefits such as Pensions Credit (which replaced the Minimum Income Guarantee in October, 2003) and Attendance Allowance for 'carers', the responses were more encouraging. One third of the respondents felt more relaxed about money. Several referred to a renewed 'dignity' or 'peace of mind' while others felt 'more comfortable' even though the monies were still not seen to be enough since little was left for luxuries (which for one household meant fish and chips) and it was still difficult to save.

Nonetheless, acquiring this extra money did help in five important areas. First, the respondents were able to spend greater weekly sums on essentials, notably food, clothing and on basic utilities to improve hygiene, comfort and avoid, for example, poor health as a result of a lack of sufficient warmth. Second, a significant proportion reported that their mobility had been enhanced by the fact that they could buy discounted bus passes or afford to use their car more often. Some could even afford to pay friends to help them and, because of this, the respondent overcame the embarrassment of having to ask for help without the offer of recompense. Third, respondents were able to make use of a wider range of goods and services. Typically, they were able to employ casual handymen, gardeners, cleaners and decorators. All, concludes Craig (2004, p 104), "were likely to impact on the social and emotional lives of respondents", since several people told of how social contact, even if it happened to be over a cup of tea at home, was of immense importance.

A fourth benefit was that many of the individuals contacted were also able to make lump-sum payments for items previously beyond their reach. Examples of which included the essential items of a mobility scooter, a down payment on a disability car, a carpet, a vacuum cleaner and a fridge. Finally, the fifth area related to personalised forms of expenditure. Due to the extra financial support, about a third of the respondents could afford presents (for children, grandchildren and friends), and thus participate in what most of us would see as an essential fabric of social intercourse.

Critically, these five areas of expenditure have shown that it is possible to improve the emotional and physical lives of the respondents. Enhanced mobility, concludes Craig, can bring increased social contact and, conversely, reduce the likelihood of isolation and depression. A better diet can "bring better health; the purchase of alarms, of important services [can contribute] to a more general sense of well-being" (Craig, 2004, p 105) and, eventually, could lead to a reduction in personal stress. Such considerations have not been fully appreciated or incorporated by New Labour. Extra payments still remain limited in both scope and in amount. Even after receiving relatively large benefit increases, Craig still found that a substantial minority studied in the survey felt they had an inadequate income to live on.

Furthermore, the persistence of means-tested benefits serves to exacerbate the situation. Despite the aforementioned evidence of a low take-up rate for means-tested benefits (Craig, 2004), stigmatisation has not been overcome with their removal. Similarly, the pertinent issues of 'participation', 'security', 'health' and 'mobility' have not been addressed in any great depth. Instead of trying to satiate the social and emotional needs of retired individuals, New Labour has retained its right of judgement and has continued with the meagre provision of 'adequate' levels of benefit through its rigid assessment for entitlement. Indeed, with this dual retention, New Labour is failing to grasp "the extent to which older people are able to operate as citizens in their own right and how an appropriate – and differentiated – definition of citizenship might be framed for them" (Craig, 2004, p 112). And with this failure, older people are being denied the fundamental citizenship rights of 'dignity', 'choice' and 'control' and the concomitant ability to participate in society on terms of their own choosing.

As before, familiar themes are being raised. Rather than allow community to evolve through interaction and develop from within, for instance, New Labour is again emulating Etzioni's communitarianism by attempting to impose its own narrowly conceived interpretations of community and social citizenship (because of its close association) upon those who do not necessarily live to, or agree with, such conceptualisations. In essence, New Labour's quest to revive a sense of community that will overcome the perceived social ills of contemporary society is destined to be ineffectual. If truth be told, New Labour is working towards a model of community that seriously lacks the fluidity to realise community can mean different things to different people at different times in different places and situations (Prideaux, 2004). As Craig (2004, p 97) stresses, the current political definitions of community and social citizenship used by New Labour suffer from "an inbuilt exclusion/inclusion tension", and, because of this, emphatically fail to address the real problems faced by individuals living outside of the paid labour market for whatever reason.

Managing the economy: a final paradox?

Finally, attention needs to return to New Labour's benevolent attitude towards capitalism, the laissez-faire market and the implicit belief that through effective management of the economy and the working environment social cohesion can be extensively created. In this respect, there exist two remaining considerations that still have to be addressed. One briefly involves the possibility that the New Deal schemes may not be fulfilling the promises that New Labour have attached to them, while the other engages with the possible strain of relative economic success.

With regard to the former, White (2000) argues that one of the preconditions of welfare contractualism (as epitomised by the New Deal conditionality principles) should be the provision of 'real' opportunities for the participants concerned. As Dwyer (2004) points out, the 1.25 million people helped back into work since the New Deals began should not be dismissed lightly. Nevertheless, Dwyer goes on to say that a number of commentators (Grover and Stewart, 2000; Gray, 2001; Peck, 2001; Prideaux, 2001) have cast doubt over the apparent success of the New Deals. By contrast, it could be that capital is the real beneficiary rather than unemployed people or lone parents not participating in the paid labour market.

Certainly it is possible to argue that the specifics of the New Deals can actually help provide lucrative gains for the unscrupulous or, equally, provide a financial 'lifeline' for struggling companies. At the level of unskilled employment, for example, the rewards that an employer would receive for recruiting a New Deal participant obviously encourages the use of 'workfare' recruits rather than full-time employees. When competition is fierce, or during times of economic recession, it hardly makes sense for many entrepreneurs to employ an individual for 36 hours per week at a cost of £151.20 (calculated on the basis of a minimum rate of £4.20 per hour) when they could pay an individual as little as £91.20 with the difference being made up from a £60 per week New Deal subsidy (Government Green Paper, 1998b, ch 3, pp 3-4). Add to this a further grant for £750 per every welfare-to-work trainee (1998b, ch 3, p 4), and it becomes clear that the use of a subsidised labour force can offer an employer a substantial incentive.

To add to the doubts, Dwyer (2004) and Peck (2001) also remark upon the unassuming job entry rates the New Deal schemes have achieved from their inception until March 2000. Overall, only a third of participants leave to enter paid work, while many of those who do leave the New Deal become trapped in 'contingent employment' in that they continually move from one short-term, low-paid and inevitably insecure job to another. Set against this backdrop, it is hard to argue that New Labour has fulfilled White's (2000) criterion of providing meaningful employment for individuals participating in the New Deal schemes. Nor is it easy to argue that such indications would deter physical or emotional feelings of alienation on behalf of the less successful participants and promote social inclusion through the revival of a sense of community and belonging.

In truth, New Labour can only be relying upon its functionalist conviction that employers and managers are inherently responsible members of society who, in the long term, will create meaningful employment opportunities through their entrepreneurial zeal and activity (see Chapters Two and Three). Yet this is a strange and incongruous attitude to hold in the light of New Labour's recounted acceptance of the basic premises behind the notion of an irresponsible 'underclass' (described in Chapter Five). Clearly, the government appear to be forwarding two different interpretations of human nature. Or is it that New Labour purports a theory of moral development? Either way the interpretations appear to be fundamentally flawed.

With specific reference to a developmental approach, it would be interesting to find out exactly when New Labour envisages that individuals stop being irresponsible and develop a moral responsibility. What happens to them to change their basic nature? Conversely, New Labour's acceptance of Murray's formative assumptions behind the concept of an 'underclass' also represent an acceptance of welfare dependency as a manifestation of calculated decision making. If it is true that the 'underclass' are capable of making such rational but avaricious decisions, then it must also be true that the rest of society are also capable of the same. In sum, the notion of two facets of human nature dividing themselves along the unemployed–entrepreneur divide simply does not stand up. Consequently, governmental faith in the employer to be responsible and act benevolently in the best interests of its employees and society as a whole represents an illogical if not a contradictory stance to adopt.

At present, however, the future looks bright for Britain on the economic front. In a review of EU finances, for instance, Brussels declared Britain's growth rate to be the third highest in the 15 nation bloc and more than double the Eurozone average of 1%. Indeed, it was predicted that the British economy would grow by 2.2% in 2003 and by 2.6% in 2004. Moreover, the commission estimated that there would also be a concomitant growth in jobs by 0.5% during 2003. This is second only to Spain and Luxembourg (Osborn, 2003). On the question of participation in the paid labour market, official figures released in 2003 revealed that unemployment was at its lowest since September 1975. According to the National Statistics Office, the figure for those claiming benefit stood at 926,900 and represented the lowest figure for some 28 years (Agence France-Presse, 2003).

All, it would seem, is well. However, economic success comes with its own problems. Paradoxically, the tasks of management and control become more difficult as the economy improves. With the characteristic provision of increased job availability in a successful economy comes a greater choice for employees. With greater choice comes the opportunity to reject specific types and conditions of employment that hitherto would have been grudgingly accepted. Certainly, recent evidence relating to the government's attempts to stem the growing shortages of teachers and nurses in Britain at present tends to stress the point quite forcibly.

In relation to teaching, for example, the government claimed, at the beginning of August 2002, it had stimulated the highest rise in the number of teachers for 20 years, while in April of the same year the Department for Education and Skills confirmed an overall drop in the number of vacant teaching posts from 1.4% to 1.2% for the year to January. At the same time, it was also stated that there was a corresponding increase of 9,400 in the number of teachers in full-time posts. Indeed, since 1997 the number of full-time qualified regular teachers had risen by 5,000 to 355,000 and the number of part-timers had gone from 28,200 to 34,500 (Smithers, 2002).

By April 2004, the figure for full-time equivalent teachers was declared by Charles Clarke (Secretary of State for Education and Skills) to be 427,800 – 28,600 more than 1997 (DfES, 2004). Apart from these figures not correlating (how can a rise of 28,600 teachers since 1997 equal 427,800 when the previous figures for 1997 suggest there were 350,000 teachers in full-time posts?), these figures obfuscate the problem of vacancies still remaining and conveniently conceal the increased use of unqualified teachers (McAvoy, 2004). Moreover, as Phil Willis (the Liberal Democratic Shadow Education Secretary) remarked back in 2002, such figures "hide the fact that 30% of new recruits leave teaching within three years, and the fact that increasing numbers of schools depend on temporary, overseas or agency staff" (cited by Smithers, 2002).

Poignantly, when 102 teachers across a range of schools were asked to give their reasons for leaving, 85.2% of the responses (which amounted to 247 in all) were overwhelmingly negative in that they referred to 'getting out' of teaching. Only 14.8% alluded to the attractions of something else (Smithers and Robinson, 2002). The situation in nursing is not dissimilar. According to the Department of Health in June 2003, there were 367,520 nurses working in the NHS. This amounted to an increase of 17,000 over the previous year and a total of 50,000 nurses that have been recruited to the NHS since 1997 (Department of Health, 2003). In spite of these encouraging figures, the Royal College of Nursing (2003) warned that up to 20,000 nurses are leaving the NHS every year while the growth of international recruitment has seen the registration of 34,000 overseas nurses to the Nursing Midwifery Council. In addition, the Royal College is also worried by the fact that some 50,000 nurses will reach retirement age by 2008 (Hall, 2003).

Clearly there is a problem over retention and the maintenance of staffing levels. Besides retirement, a member survey of the Royal College found that 26% of all respondents gave 'stress and workload' as the main reason for changing jobs within the health sector whereas the figure rose sharply to 52% for those that left the NHS altogether. In this respect, some 59% of the relevant replies cited 'dissatisfaction with previous job' as the main reason for leaving an NHS employer and working outside the sector. In sum, the Royal College of Nursing categorised the reasons for changing jobs into four main areas. The first category related to 'career factors', such as experience, promotion and future prospects. The second involved pay-related factors and the third entailed work–life balance over a change in hours and family circumstances. Last, but by no means least, the fourth category concerned negative reasons related to their previous job; that is, dissatisfaction, bullying and harassment or closure of workplace (Royal College of Nursing, 2002, pp 49-57).

As we have seen throughout the discussions of a variety of different groupings in this chapter, money is again an important aspect. However, it is not the only consideration that has to be taken into account by government and policy makers. Nurses, like teachers, are finding that the pressure of working in their respective environment is creating friction and dissatisfaction that can surmount and deter purely financial inducements to remain. In a relatively prosperous economy, as is the case today, the opportunity to leave and gain alternative employment is more readily available. Thus New Labour's emphasis upon 'paid' work is myopic to say the least.

Moreover, if the trend arising out of the fields of teaching and nursing is representative of society as a whole during an economic 'upturn', then it could well be the case that any attempt to manage a highly mobile labour force is doomed to failure by its own success. By the same token, benign faith in the capitalist system and the belief that a successful market economy can revive individual and collective responsibility through a regeneration of communal relations is also misplaced. Certainly evidence in this book has shown that social engineering based on the principles of the 'rational economic man' is not the answer. In this respect, New Labour's attempts to impose and administer its own ideas of community and social citizenship do not represent the way forward. In truth, the path taken by the present government has not managed to address the real problems in British society. Instead, New Labour has only scratched at the surface with its limited understanding and extrapolation. Nevertheless, the book has shown that this is not entirely through a failure of intention, so much as a lack of comprehension based upon outdated and oft-discredited sociological viewpoints.

By way of a contrast, Bauman (1998) possibly offers a clearer insight into the direction contemporary British society should take in light of the problems and issues raised so far. Although Bauman may well have been a little premature in his declaration that Britain is now a society based on consumption, his insinuation that the 'work ethic' has lost its relevance to notions of responsibility, community and social citizenship is of crucial importance. On its own, this fundamental realisation of a new value system should have been sufficient to render the predominant 'work-first', laissez-faire principles outmoded and inappropriate. As we have seen, this has not been the case. As a consequence, social exclusion, tension and contradiction will still permeate British society. Perhaps the final paradox emanating out of the discussions throughout this work, is that Bauman's supposedly 'utopian' advocacy for the decoupling of income entitlement from income-earning capacity (and, logically, the separation of work from the paid labour market) actually represents the most realistic solution to social exclusion after all.

Bibliography

Ackers, L. and Dwyer, P. (2002) *Senior citizenship?*, Bristol: The Policy Press.

Agence France-Presse (2003) 'British unemployment dips to fresh 28-year low', ClariNet, 12 November (quickstart.clari.net).

Albritton, R. (1999) *Dialectics and deconstruction in political economy*, Basingstoke: Palgrave.

Alexander, J. (1987) *Sociological theory since 1945*, London: Hutchinson.

Allen, V. (1975) *Social analysis: A Marxist critique and alternative*, London: Longman.

Anderson, J.-G. and Jensen, P. (eds) (2001) *Changing labour markets: Welfare policies and citizenship*, Bristol: The Policy Press.

Arnason, J. (1987) 'Figurational sociology as a counter-paradigm', *Theory, Culture & Society*, vol 4, no 4, pp 429-56.

AoC/UfI (Association of Colleges/University for Industry) (2001) *Workforce development in SMEs: A joint report by AoC and UfI on increasing the take-up of learning by small firms* (www.ufi.com/home/section4/1-summaries/smeresearch.pdf).

Auletta, K. (1982) *The underclass*, New York: Random House.

Bagihole, B. and Byrne, P. (2000) 'From hard to soft law and from equality to reconciliation in the United Kingdom', in L. Hantrais (ed) *Gendered policies in Europe: Reconciling employment and family life*, London: Macmillan, pp 124-42.

Bagguley, P. and Mann, K. (1992) 'Idle thieving bastards? Scholarly representations of the underclass', *Work, Employment and Society*, vol 6, no 1, pp 113-26.

Barlow, A. and Duncan, S. (1999) *New Labour's communitarianism, supporting families and the 'rationality mistake'*, Working Paper no 10, Leeds: Centre for Research on Family, Kinship and Childhood: University of Leeds.

Bauer, R. (1997) 'A community is a community – but in reality roses are different, and bunches much more so', *Voluntas*, vol 8, no 1, pp 70-75.

Bauman, Z. (1998) *Work, consumerism and the new poor*, Buckingham: Open University Press.

Bendix, R. and Lipset, S.M. (eds) (1967) *Class, status, and power* (2nd edn), London: Routledge Kegan Paul.

Bevir, M. and O'Brien, D. (2002) *The philosophy of John Macmurray: The moral, social and political philosophy of the British Idealists*, (www.psa.ac.uk/cps/1999/bevir2.pdf).

Blair, T. (1994) 'Sharing responsibility for crime', in A. Coote (ed) *Families, children and crime*, London: IPPR, p 90.

Blair, T. (1996) *A New Statesman special selection from New Britain: My vision of a young country*, London: The New Statesman.

Blair, T. (2000) Speech to the Annual Conference of the Women's Institute, London, 8 June.

Blair, T. (2003) 'The Third Way: New politics for the new century', in A. Chadwick and R. Heffernan (eds) *The New Labour reader*, Cambridge: Polity Press, pp 28-33.

Blau, P. (1975) *Approaches to the study of social structure*, New York: The Free Press.

Bourricaud, F. (1981) *The sociology of Talcott Parsons*, Chicago: University of Chicago Press.

Bowring, F. (1997) 'Communitarianism and morality: in search of the subject', *New Left Review*, issue 222, pp 93-113.

Broom, L. and Selznick, P. (1956) *Sociology* (2nd edn), New York: Row, Peterson and Co.

Brown, G. (1994) *Fair is efficient – A socialist agenda for fairness*, London: Fabian Tract no 563.

Brown, J. (1996) 'The focus on single mothers', in R. Lister (ed) *Charles Murray and the underclass: The developing debate*, London: IEA Health and Welfare Unit, pp 61-65.

Buxton, W. (1985) *Talcott Parsons and the capitalist nation-state*, London: University of Toronto Press.

Cammack, P. (2004) 'Giddens's way with words', in S. Hale, W. Leggett and L. Martell (eds) *The Third Way and beyond: Criticisms, futures, alternatives*, Manchester: Manchester University Press, pp 151-66.

Carter, J. (ed) (1998) *Post modernity and the fragmentation of welfare*, London: Routledge.

Chadwick, A. and Heffernan, R. (eds) (2003) *The New Labour reader*, Cambridge: Polity Press.

Clarke, J. (2004) 'Dissolving the public realm? The logics and limits of neo-liberalism', *Journal of Social Policy*, vol 33, no 1, pp 27-48.

Clarke, S. (1991) *Marx, marginalisation and modern sociology: From Adam Smith to Max Weber*, (2nd edn), Basingstoke: Macmillan.

Cohen, R., Coxall, J., Craig, G. and Sadiq-Sangster, A. (1990) *Hardship Britain*, London: Child Poverty Action Group.

Conford, P. (1996) *The personal world: John Macmurray on self and society*, Edinburgh: Floris Books.

Coote, A. (ed) (1994) *Families, children and crime*, London: IPPR.

Costello, J. (2002) *John Macmurray: A biography*, Edinburgh: Floris Books.

Craig, G. (2004) 'Citizenship, exclusion and older people', *Journal of Social Policy*, vol 33, no 1, pp 95-114.

Cuneo, C. (2000) *Talcott Parsons* (http://socserv2.mcmaster.ca/soc/courses/soc2r3/sf/parsons.htm).

Daguerre, A. with Taylor-Gooby, P. (2004) 'Neglecting Europe: explaining the predominance of American ideas in New Labour's welfare policies since 1997', *Journal of European Social Policy*, vol 14, no 1, pp 25-39.

Darwin, C. (1859) *The origin of species*, London: John Murray.

David, M. (1996) 'Fundamentally flawed', in R. Lister (ed) *Charles Murray and the underclass: The developing debate*, London: IEA Health and Welfare Unit, pp 150-5.

Davis, K. and Moore, W.E. (1967) 'Some principles of stratification', in R. Bendix and S.M. Lipset (eds) *Class, status and power* (2nd edn), London: Routledge Kegan Paul, pp 47-53.

Deacon, A. (2002) *Perspectives on welfare*, Buckingham: Open University Press.

Deacon, A. and Mann, K. (1997) 'Moralism and modernity: the paradox of New Labour thinking on welfare', *Benefits*, no 20, pp 2-6.

Deacon, A. and Mann, K. (1999) 'Agency, modernity and social policy', *Journal of Social Policy*, vol 28, no 3, pp 413-35.

Dean, H. (2002) 'Business versus families: whose side is New Labour on?', *Social Policy and Society*, vol 1, no 1, pp 3-10.

Dean, H. (2003) 'Re-conceptualising welfare-to-work for people with multiple problems and needs', *Journal of Social Policy*, vol 32, no 3, pp 441-59.

Dean, H. and Melrose, M. (1999) *Poverty, riches and social citizenship*, Basingstoke: Macmillan.

Dean, H. and Shah, A. (2002) 'Insecure families and low-paying labour markets: comments on the British experience', *Journal of Social Policy*, vol 31, no 1, pp 61-80.

Dean, H. and Taylor-Gooby, P. (1992) *Dependency culture: The explosion of a myth*, Hemel Hempstead: Harvester Wheatsheaf.

Department of Health (2003) 'Further increases in numbers of nurses and doctors working in the NHS', Press Notice 2003/0242, (www.dh.gov.uk).

Derber, C. (1995) *What's left? Radical politics in the postcommunist era*, Amherst: University of Massachusetts Press.

Dey, I. (1996) *The poverty of feminisation*, Edinburgh: University of Edinburgh Press.

DfEE (Department for Education and Employment) (2001) *Excellence in cities: Extending excellence*, London: HMSO.

DfES (Department for Education and Skills) (2004) 'More teachers in schools – Clarke', Press Notice 2004/0083 (www.dfes.gov.uk).

Driver, S. (2004) 'North Atlantic drift: welfare reform and the "third way" politics of New Labour and the New Democrats', in S. Hale, W. Legett and L. Martell (eds) *The Third Way and beyond: Criticisms, futures, alternatives*, Manchester: Manchester University Press, pp 31-47.

Driver, S. and Martell, L. (1997) 'New Labour's communitarianisms', *Critical Social Policy*, vol 17, no 3, pp 27-47.

Driver, S. and Martell, L. (1998) *New Labour: Politics after Thatcherism*, Cambridge: Polity Press.

Driver, S. and Martell, L. (2002) 'New Labour, work and the family', *Social Policy & Administration*, vol 36, no 1, pp 46-61.

Duncan, S. (2000) *New Labour's 'rationality and morality mistakes' and some alternatives*, Workshop 3, Paper no 11, Leeds: CAVA, University of Leeds.

Duncan, S. (2002) 'Policy discourses on "reconciling work and life" in the EU', *Social Policy and Society*, vol 1, no 4, pp 305-14.

Duncan, S. and Edwards, R. (1999) *Lone mothers, paid work and gendered moral rationalities*, London: Macmillan Press Ltd.

Durkheim, É. (1933) *The division of labour in society*, London: Collier-Macmillan.

Durkheim, É. (2002) *Suicide*, London: Routledge Classics.

Dwyer, P. (1998) 'Conditional citizens? Welfare rights and responsibilities in the late 1990s', *Critical Social Policy*, vol 18, no 4, pp 519-43.

Dwyer, P. (2000a) *Welfare rights and responsibilities: Contesting social citizenship*, Bristol: The Policy Press.

Dwyer, P. (2000b) 'British Muslims, welfare citizenship and conditionality: some empirical findings', *Islamic values, human agency and social policies* (RAPP Working Paper 2), Leeds: Race and Public Policy Research Unit, Department of Sociology and Social Policy, University of Leeds.

Dwyer, P. (2002) 'Making sense of social citizenship: some user views on welfare rights and responsibilities', *Critical Social Policy*, vol 22, no 2, pp 273-99.

Dwyer, P. (2004) 'Creeping conditionality in the UK: from welfare rights to conditional entitlements', *Canadian Journal of Sociology*, vol 29, no 2, pp 265-87.

Elias, N. (1970a) *Processes of state formation and nation building*, ISA Paper (www.usyd.edu.au/su/social/elias/state.html).

Elias, N. (1970b) *Was ist Soziologie?*, Munich: Juventa Verlag.

Elias, N. (1984) *The civilising process*, Oxford: Blackwell.

Ellwood, D. (1988) *Poor support: Poverty in the American family*, New York, NY: Basic Books, Inc.

Ellwood, D. and Summers, L. (1986) 'Is welfare really the problem?', *The Public Interest*, no 83, pp 57-78.

Etzioni, A. (1961) *A comparative analysis of complex organizations: On power, involvement, and their correlates*, New York: The Free Press.

Etzioni, A. (1973) 'Towards a theory of societal guidance', in E. Etzioni-Halevy and A. Etzioni (eds) *Social change: Sources, patterns, and consequences*, New York: Basic Books, pp 145-60.

Etzioni, A. (1995a) *The spirit of community: Rights, responsibilities and the communitarian agenda*, London: Fontana Press.

Etzioni, A. (1995b) 'Nation in need of community value', *The Times*, 20 February.

Etzioni, A. (1995c) 'So what's the big idea, Mr Etzioni?', Interview with B. Cambell, *The Independent*, 16 March.

Etzioni, A. (1997) *The new golden rule: Community and morality in a democratic society*, London: Profile Books Ltd.

Etzioni, A. (1998) 'A matter of balance: rights and responsibilities', in A. Etzioni (ed) *The essential communitarian reader*, Oxford: Rowman and Butterfield Publishers Inc, pp ix-xxiv.

Etzioni, A. (ed) (1998) *The essential communitarian reader*, Oxford: Rowman and Butterfield Publishers Inc.

Etzioni, A. (2000) *The third way to a good society*, London: Demos.

Etzioni-Halevy, E. and Etzioni, A. (eds) (1973) *Social change: Sources, patterns, and consequences*, New York: Basic Books Inc.

Ferré, F. (1962) '"Persons in relation" by John Macmurray: a book review', *Theology Today*, vol 19, no 2, pp 286-8.

Field, F. (1993) 'Newsnight', BBC2 (8 July), cited in K. Mann and S. Roseneil (1994) '"Some mothers do 'ave 'em": backlash and the gender politics of the underclass debate', *Journal of Gender Studies*, vol 3, no 3, pp 317-31.

Fielding, M. (2000) 'Community, philosophy and education policy: against effectiveness ideology and the immiseration of contemporary schooling', *Education Policy*, vol 15, no 4, pp 397-415.

Foucault, M. (2002) *The order of things*, London: Routledge Classics.

Fox Harding, L. (2000) *Supporting families/controlling families? Towards a characterisation of New Labour's 'family policy'* (Working Paper 21), Leeds: Centre for Research on Family, Kinship and Childhood, University of Leeds.

Gall, G. and McKay, S. (2001) 'Facing "fairness at work": union perception of employer opposition and response to union recognition', *Industrial Relations Journal*, vol 32, no 2, pp 94-113.

Gerth, H. (1997) 'On Talcott Parsons' "The Social System" edited by Michael W. Hughey', *International Journal of Politics, Culture and Society*, vol 10, no 4, pp 673-84.

Giddens, A. (1994) *Beyond Left and Right: The future of radical politics*, Cambridge: Polity Press.

Giddens, A. (1998a) *The Third Way*, Cambridge: Polity Press.

Giddens, A. (1998b) 'Beyond left and right', *The Observer*, 13 September.

Giddens, A. (2000) *The Third Way and its critics*, Cambridge: Polity Press.

Giddens, A. (2003) 'The Third Way: the renewal of social democracy', in A. Chadwick and R. Heffernan (eds) *The New Labour reader*, Cambridge: Polity Press, pp 34-8.

Gingrich, P. (1999a) 'Functionalism and Parsons' (http://uregina.ca/~gingrich/n2f99.htm).

Gingrich, P (1999b) 'Parsons (continued)' (http://uregina.ca/~gingrich/n4f99.htm).

Goode, J. and Maskowsky, J. (eds) (2001) *The new poverty studies: The ethnography of power, politics and impoverished people in the United States*, New York: New York University Press.

Gordon, D. and Pantazis, C. (1997) *Breadline Britain in the 1990s*, Aldershot: Ashgate.

Government Green Paper (1998a) *The learning age: A renaissance for a new Britain*, (February), London: DfEE.

Government Green Paper (1998b) *New ambitions for our country: A new contract for welfare*, (March) (www.dss.gov.uk).

Government Green Paper (2001) *Towards full employment in a modern society*, London: HMSO.

Government Report (1999) *Opportunity for all: Tackling poverty and social exclusion*, (First Annual Report), London: The Stationery Office.

Government White Paper (1997) *Excellence in schools* (July), London: DfEE.

Government White Paper (1998) *Fairness at work* (May), London: Department of Trade and Industry.

Government White Paper (2003) *The future of higher education* (January), London: The Stationery Office.

Graham, H. (1993) *Hardship and health in women's lives*, Hemel Hempstead: Harvester Wheatsheaf.

Gray, A. (2001) 'Making work pay – devising the best strategy for lone parents in Britain', *Journal of Social Policy*, vol 30, no 2, pp 189-207.

Grice, A. and Prescott, M. (1994) 'Blair warns Labour: we are not yet fit to govern', *The Sunday Times*, 2 October.

Grover, C. and Stewart, J. (2000) 'Modernising social security? Labour and it's welfare-to-work strategy', *Social Policy & Administration*, vol 34, no 3, pp 235-52.

Hale, S. (2002) 'Professor Macmurray and Mr Blair: the strange case of the communitarian guru that never was', *Political Quarterly*, vol 73, issue 2, pp 191-7.

Hale, S., Legett, W. and Martell, L. (eds) (2004) *The Third Way and beyond: Criticisms, futures, alternatives*, Manchester: Manchester University Press.

Hall, C. (2003) 'Nurse shortage in NHS is "near to crisis point"', *The Telegraph*, 29 April.

Hall, S., Critcher, C., Jefferson, T., Clarke, J. and Roberts, B. (1978) *Policing the crisis: Mugging the state and law and order*, Hampshire: Macmillan.

Hantrais, L. (ed) (2000) *Gendered policies in Europe: Reconciling employment and family life*, London: Macmillan.

Hamilton, P. (1983) *Talcott Parsons*, London: Tavistock.

Hamilton, P. (ed) (1985) *Readings from Talcott Parsons*, London: Tavistock.

Harrison, M. with Davis, C. (2001) *Housing, social policy and difference: Disability, ethnicity, gender and housing*, Bristol: The Policy Press.

Hayes, N. (1998) *Foundations of psychology* (2nd edn), Walton-on-Thames: Thomas Nelson.

Heron, E. (2001) 'Etzioni's spirit of communitarianism: community values and welfare realities in Blair's Britain', in R. Sykes, C. Bochel and N. Ellison (eds) *Social Policy Review*, vol 13, Bristol: The Policy Press, pp 63-87.

Heron, E. and Dwyer, P. (1999) '"Doing the right thing": Labour's attempt to forge a New Welfare Deal between the individual and the state', *Social Policy & Administration*, vol 33, no 1, pp 91-104.

Hewitt, M. (2002) 'New Labour and the redefinition of social security', in M. Powell (ed) *Evaluating New Labour's welfare reforms*, Bristol: The Policy Press, pp 189-209.

Home Office (1998) *Supporting families: A consultation document*, London: HMSO.

Home Office (1999) *Supporting families: Summary of responses to the consultation document*, London: HMSO.

Howells, K. (1996) 'Forget subsidies and second guessing the market: competition is the watchword', *The New Statesman and Society*, 7 June, p 21.

Hughes, G. and Lewis, G. (eds) (1998) *Unsettling welfare: The reconstruction of social policy*, London: Routledge.

Hughes, G. and Little, A. (1998) 'New Labour, communitarianism and the public sphere in the UK', Unpublished paper delivered at the 7th International Congress on Basic Income, Universiteit Van Amsterdam, 10-21 September.

Johnson, B. (1975) *Functionalism in modern society: Understanding Talcott Parsons*, New Jersey: General Learning Press.

Kempson, E. (1996) *Life on a low income*, York: York Publishing Services.

Kilminster, R. (1998) *The sociological revolution: From the enlightenment to the global age*, London: Routledge.

King, D. (1995) *Actively seeking work? The politics of unemployment and welfare policy in the United States and Great Britain*, London: Chicago Press Ltd.

Kingfisher, C. (ed) (2002) *Western welfare in decline: Globalization and women's poverty*, Philadelphia: University of Pennsylvania Press.

Kittay, E. (2001) 'A feminist public ethic of care meets the new communitarian family policy', *Ethics*, no 111, pp 523-47.

Labour's Economic Policy Commission (1995) *A new economic future for Britain: Economic opportunities for all* (June), London: The Labour Party.

Labour Party (1992) *It's time to get Britain working again*, London: Labour Party.

Labour Party (1997) *Labour Party Manifesto*, London: Labour Party.

Labour Party (2003) 'Labour's Business Manifesto: Equipping Britain for the future', in A. Chadwick and R. Heffernan (eds) *The New Labour reader*, Cambridge: Polity Press, pp 98-100.

Lamarck, J. (1873) *Philosophie Zoologique, ou Exposition des Considérations Relatives à L'histoire Naturelle des Aminaux*, Paris: Savy.

Lavalette, M. and Mooney, G. (2000) 'New Labour, new moralism: the welfare politics and ideology of New Labour under Tony Blair', *International Socialism*, issue 85 (http://pubs.socialistreviewindex.org.uk/isj85/lavalette.htm).

Levitas, R. (1996) 'The concept of social exclusion and the new Durkheimian hegemony', *Critical Social Policy*, vol 16, no 1, pp 5-20.

Levitas, R. (1998) *The inclusive society? Social exclusion and New Labour*, Basingstoke: Macmillan Press Ltd.

Levitas, R. (2000) 'Community, utopia and New Labour', *Local Economy*, vol 15, no 3, pp 188-97.

Levitas, R. (2001) 'Against work', *Critical Social Policy*, vol 21, no 4, pp 449-67.

Lewis, G. (1998) 'Coming apart at the seams: the crises of the welfare state', in G. Hughes and G. Lewis (eds) *Unsettling welfare: The reconstruction of social policy*, London: Routledge, pp 39-79.

Lewis, J., Polanyi, K. and Kitchin, D.K. (eds) (1935) *Christianity and the social revolution*, London: Gollancz.

Lidz,V. (1991) 'Influence and solidarity', in R. Robertson and B.Turner (eds) *Talcott Parsons:Theorist of modernity*, London: Sage Publications, pp 108-36.

Lidz,V. (2003) 'Talcott Parsons', in G. Ritzer (ed) *The Blackwell companion to major classical social theorists*, Oxford: Blackwell Publishing, pp 376-419.

Lister, R. (ed) (1996) *Charles Murray and the underclass:The developing debate*, London: IEA Health and Welfare Unit.

Lister, R. (2001) 'Citizenship and changing welfare states', in J.-G. Anderson and P. Jensen (eds) *Changing labour markets, welfare policies and citizenship*, Bristol:The Policy Press, pp 39-58.

Lukes, S. (1974) *Power: A radical view*, London: Macmillan Education Ltd.

McAvoy, D. (2004) 'Teacher numbers and class sizes – Government Release', NUT Response, 20 April, (www.teachers.org.uk).

McIntosh, E. (2001) 'The concept of the person and the future of virtue theory: Macmurray and MacIntyre', *Quodlibet Journal*, vol 3, no 4 (www.quodlibet.net/mcintosh_virtue.shtml).

McLaughlin, E.,Trewsdale, J. and McKay, N. (2001) 'The rise and fall of the UK's first tax credit: the Working Families Tax Credit 1998-2000', *Social Policy & Administration*, vol 35, no 2, pp 163-80.

McLellan, D. (ed) (1990) *Karl Marx: Selected writings*, Oxford: Oxford University Press.

Macmurray,J. (1927) 'Government by the people', *Journal of Philosophical Studies*, vol 2, pp 532-43.

Macmurray, J. (1931) 'Training the child to live', *The Listener*, vol 6, 9 December, pp 990-2.

Macmurray, J. (1932) *Freedom in the modern world*, London: Faber and Faber.

Macmurray, J. (1933a) *The philosophy of Communism*, London: Faber and Faber.

Macmurray,J. (1933b) 'The social unit', *New Britain Weekly*, 12 July.

Macmurray,J. (1933c) 'The significance of religion', *New Britain Weekly*, 2 August.

Macmurray, J. (1935a) 'Christianity and Communism: towards a synthesis', in J. Lewis, K. Polanyi and D.K. Kitchin (eds) *Christianity and the social revolution*, London: Gollancz, pp 505-26.

Macmurray, J. (1935b) *Creative society: A study of the relation of Christianity to Communism*, London: SCM Press.

Macmurray, J. (1936) *Reason and emotion*, London: Faber and Faber.

Macmurray, J. (1941) 'The community of mankind', *The Listener*, vol 26, 24 December, pp 856-7.

Macmurray, J. (1950) *Conditions of freedom*, London: Faber and Faber.

Macmurray, J. (1961) 'Persons in relation' *(The form of the personal. Vol 2)*, London: Faber and Faber.

Macmurray, J. (1965) *Search for reality in religion*, London: Allen and Unwin.

Macmurray, J. (1968) Lectures/Papers on education, Special Collections Gen 2162/2, Edinburgh: Edinburgh University Library.

Macmurray, J. (1969) 'The self as agent' *(The form of the personal. Vol 1)*, London: Faber and Faber.

Mandelson, P. and Liddle, R. (1996) *The Blair revolution*, London: Faber and Faber.

Mann, K. (1992) *The making of an English 'underclass': The social divisions of welfare and labour*, Buckingham: Open University Press.

Mann, K. (2001) *Approaching retirement: Social divisions, welfare and exclusion*, Bristol: The Policy Press.

Mann, K. and Roseneil, S. (1994) '"Some mothers do 'ave 'em": backlash and the gender politics of the underclass debate', *Journal of Gender Studies*, vol 3, no 3, pp 317-31.

Marx, K. (1848) 'The Communist Manifesto', in D. McLellan (ed) *Karl Marx: Selected writings*, (1990 edn), Oxford: Oxford University Press, pp 221-47.

Mason, J. (2004) 'Personal narratives, relational selves: residential histories in the living and telling', *Sociological Review*, vol 52, no 2, pp 139-61.

Matlay, H. and Hyland, T. (1999) 'Small firms and the university for industry: an appraisal', *Educational Studies*, vol 25, no 3, pp 253-67.

Mead, L. (1986) *Beyond entitlement*, New York: The Free Press.

Mead, L. (1987) 'The obligation to work and the availability of jobs: a dialogue', *Focus*, vol 10, no 2, pp 11-19.

Mead, L. (1988) 'Why Murray prevailed', *Academic Questions*, vol 1, no 2, pp 23-31.

Mead, L. (1991) 'The new politics of the new poverty', *Public Interest*, no 103, pp 3-20.

Merton, R.K. (1968) *Social theory and social structure* (Enlarged edn), New York: Free Press.

Millar, J. (1991) *Bearing the cost in windows of opportunity*, London: Child Poverty Action Group.

Millar, J. and Ridge, T. (2002) 'Parents, children, families and New Labour: developing family policy?', in M. Powell (ed) *Evaluating New Labour's welfare reforms*, Bristol: The Policy Press, pp 85-106.

Miller, D. and Nowak, M. (1977) *The fifties: The way we really were*, Garden City (NY): Doubleday.

Mills, C.W. (1959) *The sociological imagination*, New York: Oxford University Press.

Milne, S. (1997) 'Facts that fail to fit the figures', *The Guardian*, 16 April, p 13

Moore, J. (1988) Conservative Party Conference, Brighton: Conservative Party News Service, 12 October.

Morrison, D. (2004) 'New Labour, citizenship and the discourse of the Third Way', in S. Hale, W. Leggett and L. Martell (eds) *The Third Way and beyond: Criticisms, futures, alternatives*, Manchester: Manchester University Press, pp 167-85.

Murray, C. (1984) *Losing ground*, New York: Harper Collins.

Murray, C. (1986a) 'No, welfare isn't really the problem', *Public Interest*, no 84, pp 3-11.

Murray, C. (1986b) 'It's not fair to the children', *New Republic*, no 22, p 12.

Murray, C. (1988) *In pursuit of happiness and good government*, New York: Touchstone Books.

Murray, C. (1993) 'The coming white underclass', *The Wall Street Journal*, 29 October.

Murray, C. (1996a) 'The emerging British underclass', in R. Lister (ed) *Charles Murray and the underclass: The developing debate*, London: IEA Health and Welfare Unit, pp 23-53.

Murray, C. (1996b) 'Underclass: the crisis deepens', in R. Lister (ed) *Charles Murray and the underclass: The developing debate*, London: IEA Health and Welfare Unit, pp 99-135.

Myrdal, G. (1964) *Challenge to affluence*, London: Victor Gollancz.

Naidoo, R. and Muschamp, Y. (2002) 'A decent education for all?', in M. Powell (ed) *Evaluating New Labour's welfare reforms*, Bristol: The Policy Press, pp 145-65.

Newman, O. and de Zoysa, R. (1997) 'Communitarianism: the new panacea?', *Sociological Perspectives*, vol 40, no 4, pp 623-38.

Novitz, T. and Skidmore, P. (2001) *Fairness at work*, Oxford: Hart Publishing.

Osborn, A. (2003) 'British economy rated among strongest in EU', *Guardian Unlimited*, 9 April (www.guardian.co.uk).

Park, R. (1950) *Race and culture*, Glencoe: Glencoe Free Press.

Parker, H. (ed) (2000) *Low cost but acceptable incomes for older people*, Bristol: Family Budget Unit, Age Concern and The Policy Press.

Parsons, T. (1932) 'Economics and sociology: Marshall in relation to the thought of his time', *Quarterly Journal of Sociology*, no 46, pp 316-47.

Parsons, T. (1934a) 'Some reflections on the nature and significance of economics', *Quarterly Journal of Economics*, vol 48, no 3, pp 511-45.

Parsons, T. (1934b) 'Sociological elements in economic thought I', *Quarterly Journal of Economics*, vol 49, no 3, pp 441-53.

Parsons, T. (1935) 'The place of ultimate values in sociological theory', *International Journal of Ethics*, no 45, pp 282-316.

Parsons, T. (1937) *The structure of social action* (1st edn), New York: McGraw-Hill.

Parsons, T. (1940) 'Analytical approach to the theory of social stratification', *American Journal of Economics and Political Science*, no 6, pp 61-83.

Parsons, T. (1949) *The structure of social action* (2nd edn), Cambridge (MA): Glencoe Free Press.

Parsons, T. (1952) *The social system*, London: Tavistock Publications Ltd.

Parsons, T. (1966) *Societies: Evolutionary and comparative perspectives*, Englewood Cliffs, NJ: Prentice-Hall.

Parsons, T. (1967) *Sociological theory and modern society*, New York: Free Press.

Parsons, T. (1971) *The system of modern societies*, Englewood Cliffs, NJ: Prentice-Hall.

Parsons, T. (1985a) 'A paradigm for the analysis of social systems', in P. Hamilton (ed) *Readings from Talcott Parsons*, London: Tavistock, pp 168-78.

Parsons, T. (1985b) 'Social structure and the symbolic media of interchange', in P. Hamilton (ed) *Readings from Talcott Parsons*, London: Tavistock, pp 179-96.

Parsons, T. (1991) 'A tentative outline of American values', in R. Robertson and B.S. Turner (eds) *Talcott Parsons: Theorist of modernity*, London: Sage Publications, pp 37-65.

Parsons, T., Bales, R. and Shils, E. (1953) *Working papers in the theory of action*, New York: Free Press.

Parsons, T. and Smelser, N. (1957) *Economy and society: A study in the integration of economic and social theory*, London: Routledge and Kegan Paul.

Peck, J. (2001) 'Job alert! Shifts, spins and statistics in welfare to work policy', *Benefits*, no 30, pp 11-15.

Perrons, D. (1999) 'Flexible working patterns and equal opportunities in the European Union: conflict or compatibility?', *European Journal of Women's Studies*, vol 6, no 4, pp 391-418.

Phillips, M. (1993) *The Guardian*, 26 February, cited in K. Mann and S. Roseneil (1994) '"Some mothers do 'ave 'em": backlash and the gender politics of the underclass debate', *Journal of Gender Studies*, vol 3, no 3, pp 317-31.

Plant, R. (1993) *Social justice, Labour and the new right* (Fabian Tract 556), London: Fabian.

Powell, M. (ed) (2002) *Evaluating New Labour's welfare reforms*, Bristol: The Policy Press.

Powell, M., Exworthy, M. and Berney, L. (2001) 'Playing the game of partnership', in R. Sykes, C. Bochel and N. Ellison (eds) *Social Policy Review 13*, Bristol: The Policy Press, pp 39-61.

Prideaux, S. (2001) 'New Labour, old functionalism: the underlying contradictions of welfare reform in the US and the UK', *Social Policy & Administration*, vol 35, no 1, pp 85-115.

Prideaux, S. (2002) 'From organisational theory to the new communitarianism of Amitai Etzioni', *Canadian Journal of Sociology*, vol 27, no 1, pp 69-81.

Prideaux, S. (2004) 'From organisational theory to the Third Way: continuities and contradictions underpinning Amitai Etzioni's communitarian influence on New Labour', in S. Hale, W. Leggett and L. Martell (eds) *The Third Way and beyond: Criticisms, futures, alternatives*, Manchester: Manchester University Press, pp 128-45.

Rentoul, J. (1997) *Tony Blair*, London: Warner Books.

Ritzer, G. (2000) *Classical sociological theory*, (3rd edn), New York: McGraw Hill.

Ritzer, G. (ed) (2003) *The Blackwell companion to major classical social theorists*, Oxford: Blackwell Publishing.

Robertson, R. and Turner, B. (eds) (1991) *Talcott Parsons: Theorist of modernity*, London: Sage Publications.

Rocher, G. (1975) *Talcott Parsons and American sociology*, New York: Barnes and Noble.

Rodgers, H.R. Jr (1986) *Poor women, poor families*, New York: M.E. Sharpe.

Royal College of Nursing (2002) *Valued equally? Member Survey 2002* (www.rcn.org.uk/publications/pdf/survey-2002).

Royal College of Nursing (2003) 'RCN warns "Don't be complacent, the nursing shortage is not sorted"', Press Release, 19 September (www.rcn.org.uk/news/display.php?ID=747&area=Press).

Sadiq-Sangster, A. (1991) *Living on Income Support: An Asian experience*, London: Family Services Unit.

Selznick, P. (1953) *TVA and the grass roots: A study in the sociology of formal organization*, Los Angeles, CA: University of California Press.

Selznick, P. (1994) *The moral commonwealth*, Berkeley, CA: University of California Press.

Selznick, P. (1998) 'Social justice: A communitarian perspective', in A. Etzioni (ed) *The essential communitarian reader*, Oxford: Rowman and Butterfield Publishers Inc, pp 61-72.

Selznick, P. (1999) 'The communitarian journey', *Quadrant*, vol 23, nos 1/2, pp 19-22.

Skoble, A. (1998) 'Review: the new golden rule', *Policy*, vol 14, no 1, pp 44-6.

Smithers, A. and Robinson, P. (2002) 'Teachers leaving' (www.teachers.org.uk/resources/pdf/teachers_leaving.pdf, 18 December).

Smithers, R. (2002) 'Teacher shortage "Not taken seriously"', *The Guardian*, 6 August (www.educationguardian.co.uk/uk_news/story/ø,,769613,øø.html).

Standing, K. (1999) 'Lone mothers and "parental" involvement', *Journal of Social Policy*, vol 28, no 3, pp 479-95.

Stern, J. (2001) 'John Macmurray, spirituality, community and real schools', *International Journal of Children's Spirituality*, vol 6, no 1, pp 25-39.

Sykes, R., Bochel, C. and Ellison, N. (eds) (2001) *Social Policy Review 13*, Bristol: The Policy Press.

Timmins, N. (1996) *The five giants*, London: Fontana Press.

Titmuss, R. (1958) *Essays on the welfare state*, London: Allen and Unwin.

Tönnies, F. (1957) *Community and society* (translation and introduction by C. Loomis), East Lansing: Michigan State University Press.

Turner, J. (2003) 'Herbert Spencer', in G. Ritzer (ed) *The Blackwell companion to major classical social theorists*, Oxford: Blackwell Publishing, pp 69-92.

Ufl (University for Industry)/Learndirect (2003) 'Ufl announces new sector hub operators for national Learndirect e-learning network', (www.ufi.com, 27 August).

Van Drenth, A., Knijn, T. and Lewis, J. (1999) 'Sources of income for lone mother families: policy changes in Britain and the Netherlands and the experiences of divorced women', *Journal of Social Policy*, vol 28, no 4, pp 619-41.

Walker, A. (1996) 'Blaming the victims', in R. Lister (ed) *Charles Murray and the underclass: The developing debate*, London: IEA Health and Welfare Unit, pp 66-74.

Walker, R. (1991) *Thinking about workfare: Evidence from the USA*, London: HMSO.

Watson, D. and Bourne, R. (2001) 'Can we be excellent too? The New Labour stewardship of UK higher education', Occasional Paper, Brighton: Education Research Centre, University of Brighton.

Wetherly, P. (2001) 'The reform of welfare and the way we live now: a critique of Giddens and the Third Way', *Contemporary Politics*, vol 7, no 2, pp 149-70.

Wheatcroft, G. (1996) 'The paradoxical case of Tony Blair', *The Atlantic Online* (www.theatlantic.com/issues/96jun/blair/blair.htm).

White, S. (2000) 'Review article: social rights and social contract – political theory and the new welfare politics', *British Journal of Political Science*, no 30, pp 507-32.

Williams, B. (2001) 'What's debt got to do with it?', in J. Goode and J. Maskowsky (eds) *The new poverty studies: The ethnography of power, politics and impoverished people in the United States*, New York: New York University Press, pp 79-102.

Williams, F. (2004) *Rethinking families*, London: Calouste Gulbenkian Foundation.

Willis, P. (1977) *Learning to labour*, Farnborough: Saxon House.

Index